HowExpert Quilting Sneakers

The 50-Day Step-by-Step System to Design, Quilt, and Craft Custom Sneakers

HowExpert

For more tips related to this topic, visit HowExpert.com/quiltingsneakers.

Recommended Resources

- HowExpert.com – How To Guides on All Topics from A to Z.
- HowExpert.com/free – Free HowExpert Email Newsletter.
- HowExpert.com/books – HowExpert Books
- HowExpert.com/courses – HowExpert Courses
- HowExpert.com/clothing – HowExpert Clothing
- HowExpert.com/membership – HowExpert Membership Site
- HowExpert.com/affiliates – HowExpert Affiliate Program
- HowExpert.com/jobs – HowExpert Jobs
- HowExpert.com/writers – Write About Your #1 Passion/Knowledge/Expertise & Become a HowExpert Author.
- HowExpert.com/resources – Additional HowExpert Recommended Resources
- YouTube.com/HowExpert – Subscribe to HowExpert YouTube.
- Instagram.com/HowExpert – Follow HowExpert on Instagram.
- Facebook.com/HowExpert – Follow HowExpert on Facebook.
- TikTok.com/@HowExpert – Follow HowExpert on TikTok.

Publisher's Foreword

Dear HowExpert Reader,

HowExpert publishes quick 'how to' guides on all topics from A to Z.

Our mission is to make a positive impact in the world for all topics from A to Z…one HowExpert book at a time!

We are dedicated to creating quick, easy-to-read 'how to' guides that are structured, comprehensive, and approachable, empowering our readers to effortlessly explore and learn about their passions and interests in a meaningful and enjoyable way.

We hope our HowExpert books bring you immense value and make a positive impact on your life. Every reader, including you, plays a vital role in helping us fulfill our mission of making a positive difference in the world across all areas of interest from A to Z.

If you enjoyed one of our HowExpert guides, we would greatly appreciate it if you could take a moment to share your feedback on the platform where you discovered this book.

Thank you, and I wish you success and happiness in all aspects of your life.

To your success,

BJ Min
Founder & Publisher of HowExpert
HowExpert.com
John 14:6

COPYRIGHT, LEGAL NOTICE AND DISCLAIMER:

Table of Contents

Book Overview

HowExpert Guide to Quilting Sneakers: The 50-Day Step-by-Step System to Design, Quilt, and Craft Custom Sneakers

If you want to bring together your love for sneakers and crafting into one bold, creative journey, this is your ultimate guide. **HowExpert Guide to Quilting Sneakers** shows you how to design and quilt your own custom sneakers—combining traditional quilting skills with modern DIY footwear design.

This book isn't just about style—it's about building a real skillset, unlocking your creative potential, and producing something truly original. With a practical, easy-to-follow 50-day system, you'll learn how to turn an ordinary pair of sneakers into one-of-a-kind, handcrafted pieces of wearable art.

At the heart of this guide is the **Q-U-I-L-T-I-N-G S-N-E-A-K-E-R-S System**—a complete framework that guides you step-by-step through every stage of the process. Each letter in the acronym represents a core chapter, and each day provides focused, actionable lessons to help you build confidence, technique, and momentum.

Whether you're a quilter looking for a fresh twist, a sneaker lover wanting to express your personal style, or a creative ready to master a new craft, this book gives you the structure, tools, and inspiration to succeed.

What You'll Learn:

- **Design your sneakers from scratch** using sketches, color palettes, and mood boards
- **Select the right fabrics, sneaker bases, and tools** for both beauty and function
- **Draft, cut, and prepare quilted panels** to fit your sneakers with clean, professional alignment

- **Stitch your panels together** using essential quilting techniques and advanced options
- **Attach quilted panels securely** for durability, flexibility, and style
- **Add creative embellishments** like embroidery, layered fabric, and mixed media
- **Finish your sneakers professionally** with edge sealing, protective coatings, and polish
- **Photograph, present, and share your work** in portfolios, galleries, or online shops
- **Expand your creative scope** with matching accessories or full design collections
- **Teach, collaborate, or sell your designs** as you grow your personal or professional brand

You don't need experience in shoemaking or fashion to get started. This guide gives you everything you need to create your first pair from scratch—with clarity, encouragement, and expert-tested methods.

This isn't just a craft project. It's a full creative experience that blends artistry, expression, and hands-on design. From concept to creation, this system helps you think like a designer, quilt like an artist, and finish like a professional.

Inside the Book:

- A full **tools and materials checklist** to start with confidence
- **Printable sneaker quilting templates** for fast and accurate layout
- A clear **glossary of quilting and sneaker terms** for easy reference

- Proven **troubleshooting tips** to solve common issues and avoid mistakes

- A curated **quilted sneaker inspiration gallery** to expand your design thinking

By the end of your 50-day journey, you'll have crafted a pair of fully quilted, custom-designed sneakers—completely handmade, one-of-a-kind, and uniquely your own. You'll also walk away with the knowledge and confidence to create more designs, teach others, or build a brand around your creativity.

If you want to **design boldly, quilt confidently, and create something that's functional, fashionable, and truly original**, this guide gives you the step-by-step path to make it happen.

Start your creative journey today with **HowExpert Guide to Quilting Sneakers**—and make something no one else in the world has.

HowExpert publishes how to guides on all topics from A to Z. Visit HowExpert.com to learn more.

Introduction

Welcome to *HowExpert Guide to Quilting Sneakers*, where you'll embark on a 50-day creative journey to transform ordinary sneakers into custom, quilted masterpieces. This guide follows the **Q-U-I-L-T-I-N-G S-N-E-A-K-E-R-S System**, a step-by-step approach designed to help you learn, experiment, and express your personal style through footwear. Whether you're a complete beginner or an experienced maker, you'll develop new skills, explore advanced techniques, and build confidence as you progress each day. By the end of the journey, you'll have created your own pair of quilted sneakers—unique, functional, and reflective of your personal flair. Get ready to dive into this exciting craft and let your creativity shine!

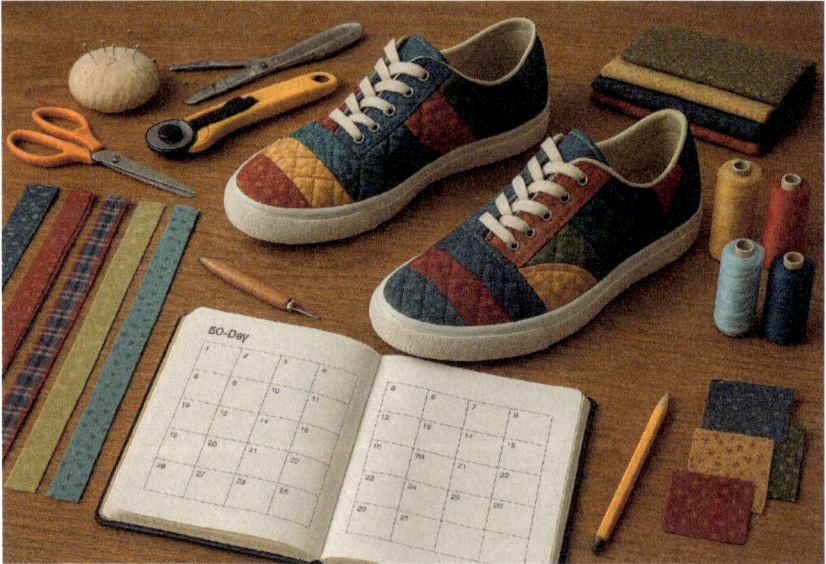

Set up an inspiring workspace with all your tools organized and ready for daily progress.

I. *Welcome to Quilting Sneakers*

Welcome to the world of quilted sneakers—a bold, colorful, and creative space where traditional craftsmanship meets personal style.

If you've ever dreamed of turning everyday footwear into something extraordinary, you're in the right place. Quilting sneakers is about more than just fabric and thread—it's about making a statement, expressing your unique identity, and transforming something ordinary into art you can wear. This book is your creative companion, here to guide you from your very first step to your final stitch.

II. Why Quilt Sneakers?

Quilted sneakers combine the warmth, texture, and visual richness of quilting with the practicality and pop culture appeal of sneakers. This fusion allows you to create wearable art that stands out. Unlike traditional quilting or standard shoe customization, quilting sneakers offers a rare intersection of fashion and function—allowing you to showcase your creativity in every step you take. It's a meditative, skill-building, and highly personal craft that can be done right from home with minimal tools and endless possibility.

There's also a deeper reward. By quilting sneakers, you're not just crafting a pair of shoes—you're crafting confidence. You're embracing originality, pushing creative limits, and stepping away from mass-produced sameness. It's one of the most fulfilling ways to wear your art and literally walk your creative journey.

III. How to Use This 50-Day System

This book follows the **Q-U-I-L-T-I-N-G S-N-E-A-K-E-R-S System**, a unique 50-day structure designed to help you make consistent, meaningful progress each day. Each letter of the acronym represents a themed chapter, and each chapter contains daily lessons that walk you through the entire process—starting with creative vision and ending with brand-building and lifelong mastery.

Here's how it works:

- Each day introduces one clear concept or task.

- You'll read, learn, and complete a hands-on step.

- The pace is manageable, with built-in momentum that keeps you inspired.

- By Day 50, you'll have created your own quilted sneakers from start to finish—and maybe even your first full collection.

To give you a quick preview, here's how the **Q-U-I-L-T-I-N-G S-N-E-A-K-E-R-S** System unfolds:

- **Q** – Quickstart Your Quilting Sneakers Journey (Days 1–3)

- **U** – Understand Essential Materials & Tools (Days 4–6)

- **I** – Inspire Your Quilted Sneaker Design (Days 7–9)

- **L** – Layout & Pattern Preparation (Days 10–12)

- **T** – Techniques for Quilting Sneakers (Days 13–15)

- **I** – Integrate Quilted Panels onto Sneakers (Days 16–18)

- **N** – Navigate Customizing & Detailing (Days 19–21)

- **G** – Guarantee Professional-Level Finishing (Days 22–24)

- **S** – Sustain & Maintain Quilted Sneakers (Days 25–27)

- **N** – Next-Level Quilted Sneaker Techniques (Days 28–30)

- **E** – Exhibit & Share Your Creations (Days 31–33)

- **A** – Advance Your Sneaker Quilting Skills (Days 34–36)

- **K** – Knowledge Sharing & Community (Days 37–39)

- **E** – Embrace Your Quilting Journey (Days 40–43)

- **R** – Reach New Heights in Sneaker Quilting (Days 44–47)

- **S** – Sustain & Scale Your Success (Days 48–50)

Each chapter builds on the last, helping you grow from curious beginner to confident sneaker quilter—with your own personal masterpiece to show for it.

You don't have to be a professional artist, quilter, or fashion designer. You just have to be curious, creative, and open to trying something new.

IV. Essential Tools & Materials Checklist

Before diving in, let's make sure you're prepared. Here are the basic tools and materials you'll want to have on hand:

Sneaker Base Options

- Canvas low tops or high tops (recommended for quilting)
- Slip-on sneakers (optional for beginners)

Fabric Supplies

- Quilting cotton, denim, or other flexible fabrics
- Fabric glue (non-toxic, flexible drying)
- Lightweight batting or interfacing

Tools & Notions

- Fabric scissors or rotary cutter
- Quilting ruler and measuring tape
- Curved needles and embroidery needles
- Heavy-duty or quilting thread
- Fabric clips or sewing pins
- Thimble (for hand stitching)
- Seam ripper
- Marking chalk or washable fabric pens

Customization Materials (Optional)

- Embroidery thread and hoop
- Beads, sequins, patches, trims
- Mixed media fabrics (lace, vinyl, felt)
- Fabric-safe paint or markers

Protective Finishing Tools

- Fabric sealant spray (water-resistant)
- Shoe trees or inserts for shaping
- Protective gloves and workspace covering

As you go through the book, you'll be introduced to each of these tools in more detail. For now, just gather what you can and prepare your workspace. The adventure begins with curiosity—and your sneakers will soon tell your story.

Chapter 1: Q – Quickstart Your Quilting Sneakers Journey

Chapter 1 starts your creative journey with **Q** in the **50-day Q-U-I-L-T-I-N-G S-N-E-A-K-E-R-S System**, focusing on **Quickstart** — the essential first step to unlocking your creative potential. Over **Day 1**, you'll discover the world of quilted sneakers, exploring the exciting fusion of quilting and sneaker culture. On **Day 2**, you'll set clear, actionable goals to guide your progress, ensuring you stay focused and motivated throughout the process. By **Day 3**, you'll create your own sneaker inspiration board, visually capturing your design ideas, fabric choices, and personal style. These first three days will help you lay a solid foundation for your quilting journey and set the stage for everything that comes next.

Start your journey with a visual board that captures your goals, ideas, and style direction.

Day 1: Discover Quilted Sneakers – An Overview

Welcome to Day 1 of your 50-day creative adventure! Today marks the beginning of a journey where your passion for design, fabric, and footwear all come together. Whether you're brand new to DIY projects or already deep in the world of quilting and sneakers, this is where you'll discover the exciting fusion of both: quilted sneakers.

Quilted sneakers are not just trendy—they're personal. They let you transform a blank sneaker canvas into something expressive, artistic, and entirely your own. You're not just making shoes—you're making a wearable story. Today, we'll explore what quilted sneakers are, what makes them special, and why you're about to fall in love with this unique form of creative expression.

Quilted sneakers are a creative fusion of function and art— explore what's possible.

A. Step-by-Step Lesson: What Are Quilted Sneakers?

1. **The Basics**

Quilted sneakers combine fabric artistry with footwear design. Imagine a pair of canvas low-tops reimagined with denim patchwork on the heel, or high-tops featuring floral quilted panels stitched onto the sides. The fabrics are padded, stitched, and customized to add dimension and design—like a mini quilt on every shoe.

2. Where Quilting Meets Sneakers

These designs use lightweight cottons, batting, embroidery thread, and careful stitching techniques to attach quilted pieces to sneaker panels. You might add geometric patterns to the toe box, or a bold checkerboard layout on the tongue. Some creators fully cover their sneakers; others add just a few statement panels. There's no one "right" way—just your way.

3. Creative Freedom Meets Function

Quilted sneakers walk the line (literally) between art and function. You can wear them, gift them, photograph them, or even start a collection. This makes them ideal for artists, crafters, fashion-forward thinkers, or anyone who wants to turn heads with something handmade.

4. No Experience Required

You don't need to be a professional artist or quilter. All you need is curiosity, the willingness to follow a step-by-step system, and the excitement to try something new. Each upcoming day will guide you with simple tasks—from selecting fabrics to stitching panels and perfecting the finish.

B. Why This Matters

By starting with this overview, you're building the vision and motivation that will carry you through the next 49 days. Understanding what quilted sneakers are helps clarify the path ahead: from learning stitches and patterns to assembling panels and showing off your final creation. This isn't just about making something cool—it's about building a new skill set, boosting your creativity, and gaining the confidence to design something wearable and personal.

C. Tips & Creative Ideas

- **Start a Style Folder**: Save photos of sneakers, quilts, colors, or textures that catch your eye. Keep it digital or physical.

- **Search Hashtags**: Try #quiltedsneakers or #diycustoms on Instagram, Pinterest, or TikTok to explore fun ideas.

- **Mix It Up**: Combine different fabrics, themes, or colors. Don't be afraid to get bold or playful.

- **Keep It Simple at First**: Start with easy shapes and small panels—you can always get more detailed later.

D. Reflection & Motivation

You've just unlocked the world of quilted sneakers—an exciting blend of style, craft, and creativity. You now know what makes this project unique, how you'll make it your own, and why this 50-day journey will be so rewarding. Tomorrow, we'll focus on setting your personal goals—so you stay inspired, focused, and ready to create something truly unforgettable.

Day 2: Set Your Sneaker Quilting Goals

Today is all about direction. Yesterday, you discovered the creative world of quilted sneakers. Now it's time to set clear, personal goals that will guide your journey. Whether you're aiming to finish one amazing pair, learn new skills, or eventually launch your own custom line, defining your goals will keep you focused, inspired, and excited to keep going.

Setting goals early helps you make the most of this 50-day system. It creates a sense of purpose behind every stitch, color choice, and design decision. Today, you'll reflect on what you want to achieve and how you'll get there.

Define clear creative goals to guide your design choices and track your progress.

A. Step-by-Step Lesson: Define Your Quilting Sneaker Goals

1. Choose Your Big Picture Goal

What's your main objective? Do you want to create one showcase-worthy pair? Start a side hustle? Develop your artistic skills? Write it down in a sentence or two. Your goal can be personal, creative, or even practical.

2. Break It Into Milestones

Once you have your big goal, divide it into 2–3 smaller checkpoints. For example:

- Finish a design sketch by Day 9
- Complete the quilting panels by Day 17
- Wear or display your finished sneakers by Day 24
  These milestones will help you stay on track without feeling overwhelmed.

3. Define Your Success Metrics

Ask yourself: What will success look like for me? It might be wearing your sneakers confidently, receiving a compliment from a friend, or simply enjoying the creative process. Keep it real and achievable.

4. Pick a Motivation Booster

Choose something that will keep you inspired—whether it's a quote, a mood board, a playlist, or a photo of someone whose style you admire. Post it somewhere visible in your workspace.

B. Why This Matters

Clear goals transform this from a casual hobby into an intentional, rewarding experience. They keep you grounded when the stitching gets tricky or the fabric doesn't behave. With defined goals, you'll be more focused, more productive, and more proud of what you've accomplished by Day 50.

C. Tips & Creative Ideas

- **Set a Time Commitment**: Even 20–30 minutes a day can lead to amazing results.
- **Be Flexible**: It's okay if your goals evolve as you explore new ideas.
- **Write It Out**: Keep your goals in a notebook or tape them near your creative space.

- **Celebrate Progress**: Don't wait for Day 50 to be proud—acknowledge small wins along the way.

D. Reflection & Motivation

By setting your personal quilting sneaker goals today, you've just given this project purpose and power. You know what you're aiming for—and you've got a roadmap to help you get there. Tomorrow, we'll bring those goals to life visually by creating a powerful inspiration board to fuel your creativity.

Day 3: Create Your Sneaker Inspiration Board

Today is all about visualizing your ideas and bringing your creative vision to life through an inspiration board. Whether digital or physical, an inspiration board is a powerful tool to clarify your style, organize your thoughts, and keep you creatively focused throughout your quilting sneaker journey. By the end of today, you'll have a collection of images, colors, fabrics, and textures that excite and inspire you—something you can return to every time you sit down to work on your sneakers.

This step is where imagination meets planning. You've set your goals—now it's time to build a visual map to guide your designs, fabric choices, and overall aesthetic.

Use an inspiration board to stay visually aligned with your design vision and theme.

A. Step-by-Step Lesson: Build Your Sneaker Inspiration Board

1. Choose Your Format

Decide whether you want to create a **digital inspiration board** (using tools like Pinterest, Canva, or a photo folder) or a **physical board** (with magazine clippings, fabric swatches, and photos pinned to a corkboard or taped to a notebook page). Choose the format that fits your workflow and style.

2. Gather Visuals

Search for images of quilted sneakers, patchwork designs, sneakers you love, bold color palettes, textures, quilting patterns, or anything else that sparks your interest. Don't overthink it—just collect what draws your eye. Aim for at least 10–15 images.

3. Highlight Fabrics and Colors

Add fabric swatches, screenshots, or samples of colors you're considering. If you have physical fabric on hand, lay it out next to your sneaker base or tape it to your board. Pay attention to patterns (floral, geometric, abstract) and the mood they create.

4. Add Design Elements

Include shapes, motifs, or small sketches that reflect your vision. You might add a stitched heart, zigzag line, checkerboard pattern, or favorite quilt block style. This will help you develop a cohesive look as you move forward.

5. Organize and Refine

Arrange your board in a way that makes sense visually. Group by color, material, or design idea. Label favorite elements if needed. This isn't about perfection—it's about clarity and inspiration.

B. Why This Matters

Your inspiration board is more than just a collage—it's your creative compass. It will guide your design decisions, fabric choices, and layout ideas throughout the entire process. On days when you feel unsure or creatively stuck, your board will remind you of your original vision and bring you back to what excites you most about this project.

C. Tips & Creative Ideas

- **Use Color Palettes**: Pick a 3–5 color palette that reflects the look you're going for. It keeps your design consistent.

- **Layer Textures**: Include lace, denim, canvas, corduroy, or metallics to explore mixed materials.

- **Add Words or Quotes**: Paste or write a few words that represent your style: "Bold," "Cozy," "Funky," "Minimal," etc.

- **Make It Portable**: If physical, create it in a sketchbook or journal so you can take it with you.

D. Reflection & Motivation

Today you created a visual roadmap for your creative journey. Your inspiration board is a direct expression of your style, personality, and imagination—and it will serve you every step of the way. Tomorrow, we'll explore quilt patterns that can bring those ideas to life and help you shape your final design. You're on a roll—keep that momentum going!

Chapter 1 Review: Q – Quickstart Your Quilting Sneakers Journey

Chapter 1 covered **Days 1–3** of your journey through the 50-Day **Q-U-I-L-T-I-N-G S-N-E-A-K-E-R-S** system, focusing on **Q – Quickstart Your Quilting Sneakers Journey**. These opening days helped you build a strong creative foundation by introducing what quilted sneakers are, setting clear goals, and gathering inspiration to fuel your designs.

Day 1 – Discover Quilted Sneakers – An Overview

- **Understand what quilted sneakers are** – Learn how quilting techniques are applied to sneakers for texture, color, and artistic flair.

- **Explore styles and possibilities** – From full-coverage panels to small stitched details, you saw how diverse and personal each pair can be.

- **Embrace accessibility** – No experience necessary—just creativity, curiosity, and a willingness to try something new.

- **Recognize the fusion of form and function** – These sneakers are both wearable and expressive pieces of art.

Day 2 – Set Your Sneaker Quilting Goals

- **Define your purpose** – Decide whether you're creating for fun, fashion, gifts, or a potential side hustle.

- **Set realistic and motivating goals** – Whether it's completing one pair or launching a full collection, you wrote down clear intentions.

- **Visualize success** – Envision how your finished project will look, feel, and be used or shared.

- **Build direction** – Your goals will serve as a creative compass throughout the rest of the 50-day system.

Day 3 – Create Your Sneaker Inspiration Board

- **Gather visual inspiration** – Collect fabrics, colors, patterns, themes, and designs that resonate with you.

- **Organize your ideas** – Use physical pinboards, digital collages, or sketchbooks to keep your vision focused.

- **Connect with your aesthetic** – Begin to understand your unique design style and creative preferences.

- **Lay the groundwork for your first design** – This board becomes a guiding resource when it's time to sketch and build your sneakers.

With a clear understanding of quilted sneakers, a strong goal, and a custom inspiration board, you've officially jumpstarted your creative journey. In **Chapter 2: U – Understand Essential Materials & Tools (Days 4–6)**, you'll dive into the practical side—selecting fabrics, sneaker bases, and the right tools to bring your vision to life.

Chapter 2: U – Understand Essential Materials & Tools

Chapter 2 starts with **U**—which stands for **Understand**—in the **50-day Q-U-I-L-T-I-N-G S-N-E-A-K-E-R-S System**, focusing on the essential materials and tools you'll need to bring your quilted sneaker vision to life. Over the next three days, you'll tackle key steps: **Day 4** helps you select the right fabrics for your design, **Day 5** guides you in choosing the ideal sneaker base, and **Day 6** ensures you gather all the necessary quilting tools and supplies. These foundational steps will equip you with everything you need to confidently proceed with your sneaker quilting journey.

Understanding your materials sets the foundation for durable and stylish quilted sneakers.

Day 4: Select the Right Fabrics for Sneaker Quilting

Today's focus is all about fabric—the foundation of every great quilted sneaker design. The materials you choose will directly impact your sneakers' appearance, texture, flexibility, and durability. Whether you want something vibrant, vintage, bold, or soft, this step is where your creative vision starts becoming real.

Sneaker quilting requires a smart balance between aesthetics and function. You'll be working with curves, contours, and limited space, so choosing the right fabric types and qualities will set you up for success from Day 1 of actual construction.

Choose breathable, flexible fabrics that contour to the shape of sneakers without bulk.

A. Step-by-Step Lesson: Choosing the Right Fabrics

1. **Start with Lightweight Cottons**

Quilting cotton is the most popular choice for beginners—it's lightweight, flexible, easy to stitch, and comes in endless colors and prints. It holds up well when layered with batting and won't make your sneakers feel bulky or stiff.

2. Add Texture and Personality

Consider mixing in small amounts of textured fabric like denim, canvas, velvet, or corduroy for contrast. Use these sparingly as accent panels—they can add bold texture without overwhelming the design.

3. Avoid Heavy or Slippery Materials

Steer clear of thick upholstery fabrics or anything too stretchy or slick (like silk or satin). These are difficult to shape around a sneaker and can lead to bunching or uneven stitching.

4. Consider Wear and Tear

Since you'll actually be wearing these sneakers, choose fabrics that can handle movement and friction. Pre-washed cottons and tightly woven materials tend to be more durable and longer-lasting.

5. Test the Fabric on Your Sneaker Base

Before committing, cut small test swatches and drape them over your sneaker. See how they curve around the toe box, how they fold at the seams, and how they look next to your laces and sole.

B. Why This Matters

Fabric is the soul of your quilted sneaker design. Picking the right material affects not only how your shoes look—but how they feel, wear, and hold up over time. This step gives you the foundation to build sneakers that are both stylish and wearable.

C. Tips & Creative Ideas

- **Use Scrap Quilting Packs**: Pre-cut bundles often include coordinating fabrics in fun patterns.

- **Try Theme-Based Prints**: Florals, geometric shapes, retro patterns, or favorite colors make your sneakers truly your own.

- **Keep It Balanced**: Use bold prints for small panels and solids for larger areas to avoid visual clutter.

- **Pre-Wash Fabrics**: This prevents shrinking or bleeding when your shoes get wet or are cleaned.

D. Reflection & Motivation

You've just taken a huge step toward customizing your sneakers with fabric that reflects your unique style. Tomorrow, you'll focus on selecting the perfect sneaker base to match your creative vision and ensure your materials and shoes work together seamlessly. Keep the momentum going—your quilted sneaker masterpiece is starting to take shape!

Day 5: Choose Your Ideal Sneaker Base

Now that you've chosen your fabrics, it's time to pick the canvas—literally. Today, you'll choose the ideal sneaker base to serve as the foundation for your quilting masterpiece. This step is about finding a shoe that fits your style, works well with fabric application, and gives you the best results for comfort and creativity.

The right sneaker makes all the difference. Not all shoes are created equal for quilting, so today's task is to learn what works, what doesn't, and how to pick the perfect pair for your design and goals.

Canvas Low Tops	High Tops	Slip-Ons
Versatile, easy to quilt	More coverage area	Simple, smooth style

Select a sneaker base that complements your quilt design and supports secure stitching.

A. Step-by-Step Lesson: Select Your Sneaker Base

1. Start with a Simple Canvas Sneaker

Look for plain canvas sneakers with minimal logos or embellishments. These are easiest to cover, stitch onto, or glue quilted panels over. Classic styles like Vans, Converse, or generic canvas brands are great starting points.

2. Check the Structure and Flexibility

Your sneaker should be flexible enough to bend and move as you apply quilted pieces. Avoid sneakers with rigid overlays, thick padding, or lots of hardware. You want clean surfaces that are easy to measure, cut, and wrap around.

3. Low-Top vs. High-Top

Low-tops offer easier access and faster projects—great for beginners. High-tops provide more surface area for creative panels and bold quilting. Choose what matches your comfort level and vision.

4. Consider the Color

White, beige, or black bases are neutral and make fabrics pop. But you can also go bold—just make sure the base color works well with your selected fabrics and design.

5. Test Fabric Placement Before You Commit

Drape some of your chosen fabrics over different sneaker styles while shopping or before finalizing your pick. This gives you a real sense of what the final piece will look and feel like.

B. Why This Matters

The sneaker base is the literal and creative foundation of your project. Choosing the wrong shoe can lead to frustration later on— uneven surfaces, tricky stitching areas, or a design that just doesn't land. Taking the time today to find the right base sets you up for smooth, successful quilting in the days ahead.

C. Tips & Creative Ideas

- **Buy an Extra Pair**: If budget allows, grab a backup pair to experiment or create a second version later.
- **Thrift or Upcycle**: Use old sneakers with solid structure to reduce waste and add character.
- **Remove the Laces**: It's easier to work without them in for patterning and stitching.
- **Photograph Your Base**: Take a few angles of your sneaker to help with tomorrow's planning and patterning.

D. Reflection & Motivation

You've just chosen the core of your quilted sneaker project. With your fabrics selected and your sneaker base in hand, you now have all the creative elements ready to begin construction. Tomorrow, we'll gather the essential tools and supplies to bring it all together— so you're fully prepared for stitching, cutting, and assembling with confidence.

Day 6: Gather Essential Quilting Tools & Supplies

Today is all about preparation. You've selected your fabrics and your ideal sneaker base—now it's time to gather the tools that will help you bring your quilted sneaker vision to life. Having the right supplies on hand makes the entire process smoother, more enjoyable, and more professional.

Think of this as building your creative toolkit. With these items ready to go, you'll feel confident and capable every time you sit down to work. Today's goal is to make sure you're fully equipped to begin quilting, customizing, and assembling your sneakers in the days ahead.

Gathering the right tools in advance ensures smoother, more confident crafting sessions.

A. Step-by-Step Lesson: Build Your Quilted Sneaker Toolkit

1. Basic Quilting Tools

Start with essentials like fabric scissors, a rotary cutter and cutting mat (for clean, straight cuts), quilting rulers, and pins or fabric clips. These tools help you accurately measure and cut your quilt panels.

2. Needles and Thread

Get a mix of **hand-sewing needles** and **embroidery needles** for detailed stitching. For thread, choose strong cotton or polyester thread that complements your fabric colors. Embroidery floss can also be used for decorative stitches.

3. Sewing Machine (Optional but Helpful)

A basic sewing machine speeds up piecing quilt panels and reinforcing seams. While many steps can be done by hand, a machine is helpful for quicker results and stronger stitching—especially on layered fabrics.

4. Batting or Padding Material

Thin quilt batting gives your panels that soft, puffy texture. Choose low-loft batting so the sneakers don't get bulky. Fusible interfacing can also add structure to your quilted pieces.

5. Fabric Glue or Shoe Adhesive

Fabric glue or specialized shoe glue (like E6000 or Shoe Goo) helps you attach panels cleanly and securely. You'll use these to reinforce edges, corners, or sections that are harder to sew.

6. Marking Tools

Use washable fabric pens, chalk pencils, or air-erasable markers to outline cuts, stitch lines, or quilt shapes directly onto fabric.

7. Optional Embellishments

If you plan to personalize with extras, gather embroidery floss, iron-on patches, studs, buttons, or decorative trims now. It's better to have them ready before final assembly.

B. Why This Matters

Having all your tools in one place prevents delays and builds creative momentum. Instead of pausing mid-project to hunt for supplies, you'll be free to focus on your design, stitching, and assembly. These tools are your support system—helping you execute ideas with precision and ease.

C. Tips & Creative Ideas

- **Create a Dedicated Kit**: Store everything in a shoebox, bin, or tote labeled just for your quilting sneaker project.

- **Test Tools Before You Begin**: Try out scissors, pens, and adhesives on scrap fabric.

- **Label Fabrics and Supplies**: Keep small pieces organized by color or section.

- **Shop Mindfully**: Many quilting tools can be reused for future craft projects—think long-term!

D. Reflection & Motivation

Today, you've built your creative toolkit—the physical foundation of your quilting sneaker journey. With fabrics, sneakers, and tools in hand, you're fully prepared to move into pattern-making, stitching, and assembly. Tomorrow, you'll dive into design inspiration as we explore quilt patterns that work perfectly on sneakers. You're officially ready to bring your vision to life!

Chapter 2 Review: U – Understand Essential Materials & Tools

Chapter 2 covered **Days 4–6** of your journey through the 50-Day **Q-U-I-L-T-I-N-G S-N-E-A-K-E-R-S** system, focusing on **U – Understand Essential Materials & Tools**. This chapter gave you the knowledge and confidence to choose the best supplies for sneaker quilting—from fabric selection to sneaker styles and the essential tools needed to build your first custom pair.

Day 4 – Select the Right Fabrics for Sneaker Quilting

- **Learn what fabrics work best** – Focus on materials like cotton, denim, canvas, and batik for structure, comfort, and visual appeal.

- **Understand texture and weight** – Choose fabrics that are durable yet flexible enough to conform to sneaker curves.

- **Explore creative options** – Mix prints, colors, and upcycled fabrics to personalize your design.

- **Prep your fabric correctly** – Wash, press, and stabilize your fabric for clean cuts and quality results.

Day 5 – Choose Your Ideal Sneaker Base

- **Understand sneaker structure** – Learn about sneaker parts (toe box, vamp, heel tab) to better plan your quilted panel placements.

- **Pick the best base style** – Low-tops, high-tops, slip-ons—choose a style that complements your design goals and comfort level.

- **Look for custom-friendly materials** – Opt for canvas or textile-based sneakers that are easier to stitch, glue, or embellish.

- **Plan for fit and wearability** – Make sure the sneakers are the right size and shape for actual wear once customized.

Day 6 – Gather Essential Quilting Tools & Supplies

- **Build your toolkit** – Must-haves include fabric scissors, rotary cutters, cutting mats, quilting rulers, pins, needles, and thimbles.

- **Stock up on adhesives and stitch gear** – Use fabric glue, heavy-duty thread, embroidery floss, and hand-sewing needles or curved upholstery needles.

- **Add optional upgrades** – Consider stencils, fabric markers, heat erasable pens, or mini irons for extra precision.

- **Stay organized** – Set up a workspace with storage for swatches, notions, and in-progress panels.

With the right materials and tools in hand, you're fully prepared to move from planning into action. In **Chapter 3: I – Inspire Your**

Quilted Sneaker Design (Days 7–9), you'll begin sketching, exploring patterns, and developing a sneaker concept that reflects your unique creative style.

Chapter 3: I – Inspire Your Quilted Sneaker Design

Chapter 3 introduces **I**—which stands for **Inspire**—in the **50-day Q-U-I-L-T-I-N-G S-N-E-A-K-E-R-S System**, and it's all about unlocking your creativity. In these next three days, you'll explore various quilt patterns, sketch your unique sneaker concepts, and finalize your design plan. **Day 7** will guide you through exploring classic and modern quilt patterns to inspire your design, while **Day 8** focuses on sketching out your ideas to bring your vision to life. Finally, **Day 9** will help you refine your design by combining your sketches with fabric choices and stitching details, setting the stage for your first steps into quilting sneakers. This chapter is about turning your inspiration into tangible designs that reflect your unique style.

Let your sneaker ideas take shape through sketches, references, and color experimentation.

Day 7: Explore Classic & Modern Quilt Patterns

Design starts with inspiration—and today is your chance to explore the rich world of quilt patterns to find styles that match your vision. From timeless classics to bold modern styles, quilting offers a huge variety of visual textures and layouts that translate beautifully onto sneakers.

This step is about identifying what speaks to you. You don't need to be a quilting expert—just someone who can recognize what looks exciting, fun, or meaningful. The right pattern will give your sneaker design structure, personality, and creative energy.

Explore a variety of quilting patterns to match your sneaker's shape and personality.

A. Step-by-Step Lesson: Choose a Quilt Pattern That Inspires You

1. **Understand Classic Patterns**

Traditional quilt patterns like **Log Cabin, Flying Geese, Nine Patch**, and **Herringbone** are made of simple shapes (mostly squares and triangles) arranged in repeating layouts. These are great for beginners because they're easy to scale and adapt to small areas like sneaker panels.

2. Look at Modern Interpretations

Modern quilt patterns tend to use bold colors, asymmetry, negative space, or irregular block layouts. Designs like **Improv Quilting** or **Modern Stripes** give your sneaker a fresh, trendy look and feel less rigid than classic styles.

3. Match Patterns to Sneaker Zones

Smaller patterns work great on curved areas like the toe box or around the heel. Larger block designs are better for the sides or tongue. Consider how the pattern can "flow" across the shoe as you move.

4. Use Pre-Made Templates for Guidance

Search online or in quilting books for printable patterns or block layouts that you can resize and adapt. You don't need to invent something from scratch—start with a structure and customize it with fabric and color.

5. Collect Favorites into Your Style Folder

Add screenshots, sketches, or links of patterns you love into your inspiration board or notebook. Label them with ideas like "Tongue Design" or "Heel Accent" so you can reference them later.

B. Why This Matters

Exploring quilt patterns gives you structure for your creativity. Instead of starting from a blank page, you're pulling from centuries of visual tradition and putting your own twist on it. A strong pattern choice brings your sneakers together and gives each panel purpose and cohesion.

C. Tips & Creative Ideas

- **Try a Mashup**: Combine elements of two patterns (like a grid base with diagonal strips).

- **Use Color to Modernize**: A classic pattern in neon or metallic fabric feels instantly fresh.

- **Keep It Small**: Adapt patterns to scale—don't use a 12" block design on a 2" space.

- **Start Simple**: Geometric lines, checkerboards, or stripes are beginner-friendly and impactful.

D. Reflection & Motivation

Today you've unlocked the visual language of quilting. The patterns you explore now will serve as the framework for your design—and your expression. Tomorrow, you'll begin translating these ideas into sketches that map out how your sneaker will come together. You're not just making something—you're designing something that's truly yours.

Day 8: Sketch Your Quilted Sneaker Concepts

Today is all about turning inspiration into a tangible design. It's time to sketch your quilted sneaker concept—a visual plan that brings together your patterns, fabrics, and sneaker base into one cohesive idea. You don't need to be an artist to sketch—this is about clarity, not perfection. Your sketch will serve as a creative roadmap for the construction phase.

By the end of today, you'll have a rough draft of your quilted sneaker layout, showing how each panel will be designed, where fabrics will go, and how your chosen quilt patterns will come to life on your shoes.

Use progressive sketching to refine your quilt layout and choose stitch-friendly designs.

A. Step-by-Step Lesson: Sketch Your Sneaker Design

1. Use a Printable Sneaker Template

Start with a blank outline of a sneaker—either drawn by hand or printed from an online template. Look for side views, top views, and tongue overlays. This gives you a realistic canvas to work on.

2. Block Out Fabric Zones

Lightly sketch in where each section of fabric will go: toe box, sides, tongue, heel, collar, etc. Use light pencil so you can adjust and erase easily. Label the zones if needed.

3. Draw Quilt Pattern Placement

Inside each fabric section, sketch your chosen quilt pattern layout—stripes, checkerboard, triangle blocks, etc. Keep it simple; you're mapping the concept, not drawing every stitch.

4. Add Color or Texture References

Use colored pencils, markers, or fabric swatches to indicate which fabrics go where. You can also write notes directly on the sketch about materials, thread choices, or design ideas for each part.

5. Create a Sketch for Each Shoe (Optional)

If you're doing asymmetrical designs, make a sketch for each sneaker (left and right). Otherwise, one general concept sketch is enough for mirrored designs.

B. Why This Matters

Your sketch is your blueprint. It helps you visualize your design before cutting fabric or stitching anything. This step reduces guesswork, avoids mistakes, and boosts your confidence when it's time to start assembling. Even a rough draft gives you a strong creative direction moving forward.

C. Tips & Creative Ideas

- **Keep a Design Journal**: Store sketches, fabric notes, and ideas in one place for easy access.

- **Outline Stitching Plans**: Use dotted lines or arrows to show where you'll stitch or layer panels.

- **Use Digital Tools**: Try free apps like Procreate, Canva, or even PowerPoint for digital sketching.

- **Try a Mini Version**: Sketch a tiny version of your sneaker to experiment with alternate color schemes.

D. Reflection & Motivation

You've just brought your quilted sneaker design to life on paper. From a blank template to a personalized, mapped-out concept—you now have a clear vision to guide your next steps. Tomorrow, we'll finalize your design plan and make sure everything is ready for cutting, quilting, and assembling. Your creation is getting real—and it's looking amazing already!

Day 9: Finalize Your Sneaker Design Plan

Today, you'll bring everything together—your fabrics, patterns, sneaker base, and sketches—into one finalized sneaker design plan. This is the blueprint that will guide you through the hands-on stages of cutting, stitching, and assembling. With a clear plan in place, you'll move into the construction phase with confidence and clarity.

The goal isn't perfection—it's preparedness. Finalizing your plan means making informed creative decisions before you start working with physical materials. It's your personal game plan for transforming vision into wearable art.

Finalize your design plan by combining sketch, fabric selection, and stitching notes in one place.

A. Step-by-Step Lesson: Lock In Your Design Details

1. Review Your Sketches and Materials

Lay out your sneaker sketches, chosen fabrics, and quilt pattern references. Double-check that everything works together visually—color combinations, fabric textures, and overall layout.

2. Make Final Adjustments

Tweak your sketch as needed. Maybe you swap a fabric for something that fits better, adjust the pattern size, or simplify a panel to make sewing easier. This is your last chance to refine before cutting.

3. Create a Fabric Map

Write a simple breakdown of which fabric goes on which sneaker panel (e.g., "toe box: floral cotton," "heel: navy denim," etc.). This makes the assembly process faster and helps prevent mistakes.

4. Decide on Your Stitching Style

Choose whether you'll hand-sew or machine-stitch each section. Mark where you'll use decorative stitches, quilting lines, or reinforcement seams. This gives you a plan for both aesthetics and durability.

5. Set a Timeline (Optional)

If you like structure, divide your project into mini goals—like "cut and piece panels by Day 12" or "stitch and attach panels by Day 18." This helps keep your momentum going.

B. Why This Matters

Finalizing your design now prevents costly mistakes later. It saves time, reduces fabric waste, and ensures your creative decisions are intentional and aligned with your goals. You've come this far with inspiration and planning—this final step bridges the gap between vision and execution.

C. Tips & Creative Ideas

- **Photograph Your Final Plan**: Keep a digital backup in case your sketch gets lost or smudged.

- **Make a Mini Swatch Card**: Tape small fabric scraps to a page labeled with where each will go.

- **Set Up a Workspace**: Clear a dedicated area where you can start quilting and assembling tomorrow.

- **Trust Your Gut**: If something doesn't feel right in the plan, take a moment to change it—this is your art.

D. Reflection & Motivation

Today, you finalized your creative plan—and that means you're officially ready to begin making your quilted sneakers. With a clear design, mapped-out materials, and stitching strategy, you've built a strong foundation. Tomorrow, we'll start with measurements and pattern preparation so you can begin crafting with confidence. You're ready—let's build something amazing!

Chapter 3 Review: I – Inspire Your Quilted Sneaker Design

Chapter 3 covered **Days 7–9** of your journey through the 50-Day **Q-U-I-L-T-I-N-G S-N-E-A-K-E-R-S** system, focusing on **I – Inspire Your Quilted Sneaker Design**. This chapter was all about creativity, vision, and intentional design. You explored quilt patterns, turned ideas into sketches, and crafted a clear plan for your first pair of quilted sneakers.

Day 7 – Explore Classic & Modern Quilt Patterns

- **Study foundational quilt styles** – Learn traditional patterns like log cabin, flying geese, and nine-patch, and how they can be adapted for sneakers.

- **Experiment with modern interpretations** – Try asymmetry, bold color blocking, or minimalist lines for a fresh twist.

- **Match patterns to sneaker zones** – Choose patterns that work well for small curved areas like the toe, heel, or sides.

- **Balance structure and creativity** – Let tradition guide your choices while making the design your own.

Day 8 – Sketch Your Quilted Sneaker Concepts

- **Visualize your ideas** – Turn inspiration into rough sneaker sketches, focusing on layout, color, and panel placement.

- **Use templates or draw freestyle** – Either trace from a sneaker outline or sketch by hand—both help refine your vision.

- **Explore multiple versions** – Create several sketches to test combinations of patterns, fabrics, and details.

- **Capture your style direction** – Your sketches become the blueprint for the sneaker-building phase ahead.

Day 9 – Finalize Your Sneaker Design Plan

- **Commit to a design** – Choose the quilt patterns, fabrics, color palette, and sneaker base you'll use for your project.

- **Create a reference board or worksheet** – Organize swatches, stitch ideas, and design notes for easy access during production.

- **Identify construction steps** – Plan which panels to quilt, how they'll be attached, and what order to assemble them.

- **Prepare to bring your vision to life** – With your design plan in hand, you're ready to transition from concept to creation.

By the end of Chapter 3, you've done more than imagine—you've designed. Your ideas now have shape, structure, and intention. In **Chapter 4: L – Layout & Pattern Preparation (Days 10–12),** you'll take the next step by measuring, drafting, and cutting your quilted pieces with precision. Your vision is about to become reality.

Chapter 4: L – Layout & Pattern Preparation

Chapter 4 introduces **L**—which stands for **Layout**—in the **50-day Q-U-I-L-T-I-N.G S-N-E-A-K-E.R.S System**. In this chapter, you'll take your designs from inspiration to tangible creation. Over the next three days, you'll learn how to measure your sneaker base accurately on **Day 10**, ensuring that every quilted panel fits perfectly. **Day 11** will guide you through drafting and creating custom quilt patterns that match the shape and flow of your sneakers. Finally, **Day 12** focuses on precisely cutting and prepping your quilt fabrics, making sure all your materials are ready for the next phase. This chapter lays the groundwork for successful quilting by ensuring your patterns are accurately measured and crafted.

Lay the groundwork with precise measuring and pattern planning to ensure a professional fit.

Day 10: Measure Your Sneaker Base Accurately

Today's task is all about precision. You're about to move from design into hands-on creation—and that starts with accurately measuring your sneaker base. Proper measurements ensure your quilted panels fit cleanly and professionally over the shoe, avoiding awkward bunching, misaligned patterns, or loose edges.

Think of this as building the foundation for construction. The better your measurements today, the smoother your quilting and assembly will be in the coming days.

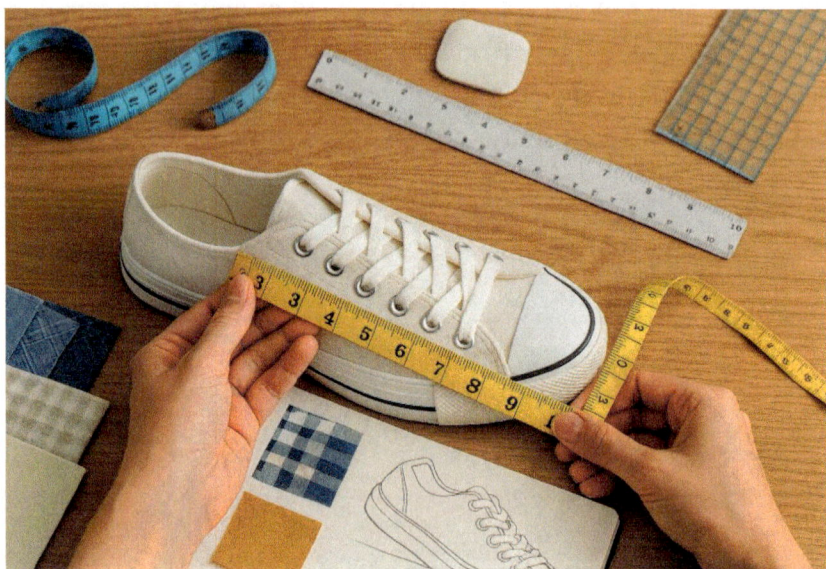

Accurate sneaker measurements are key to drafting quilt panels that wrap cleanly and snugly.

A. Step-by-Step Lesson: Measure Like a Maker

1. Remove Laces and Clean the Surface

Take the laces out of your sneakers and gently wipe them down. A clean, unobstructed surface helps you get accurate measurements and visualize fabric placement more clearly.

2. Identify Key Zones

Break the sneaker into sections: toe box, side panels, tongue, heel, collar, and back strip. You'll be measuring each one individually, as no two areas are shaped exactly alike.

3. Use Flexible Measuring Tools

Use a soft measuring tape, tailor's tape, or even a piece of string marked with a ruler. This helps you wrap around curves and edges more accurately than a rigid ruler.

4. Record Length and Height for Each Section

Measure both the **length and height** (or width) of each section. For example, the side panel might be 5 inches long and 2 inches high. Record all dimensions in a notebook or sketch next to your design drawing.

5. Trace or Template If Needed

For curved or irregular sections (like the toe box), create a rough paper template by placing tracing paper or scrap fabric directly over the area and outlining it. Cut it out and test the fit.

B. Why This Matters

Accurate measurements are the difference between a quilted sneaker that looks homemade and one that looks custom-made. This step gives you a reliable foundation for cutting and piecing quilt panels that look clean, professional, and polished.

C. Tips & Creative Ideas

- **Measure Twice**: Double-check every measurement to avoid cutting mistakes later.

- **Label Each Section**: Mark your notes with "Left Side Panel," "Right Heel," etc., to stay organized.

- **Use a Sneaker Photo**: Print or draw an outline of your sneaker and write the measurements on each section.

- **Test with Scrap Paper**: Cut paper pieces to match your measurements and tape them to your sneaker to visualize placement.

D. Reflection & Motivation

Today you laid the groundwork for a flawless fit. Your measurements will shape every cut, stitch, and panel from here on out. With accuracy on your side, you're ready to start creating custom patterns that bring your design to life. Tomorrow, we'll begin drafting those patterns to match your sneaker's unique shape—your project is officially in motion!

Day 11: Draft & Create Sneaker Quilt Patterns

With your sneaker measurements in hand, today's focus is drafting custom quilt patterns that will fit each section of your sneaker. This step transforms your design sketch into real, functional templates you'll use to cut fabric with precision. Think of it as creating the puzzle pieces that will bring your sneakers to life.

Even if you've never made a pattern before, don't worry—this process is simple when broken into steps. All you need is paper, scissors, your measurements, and a little patience.

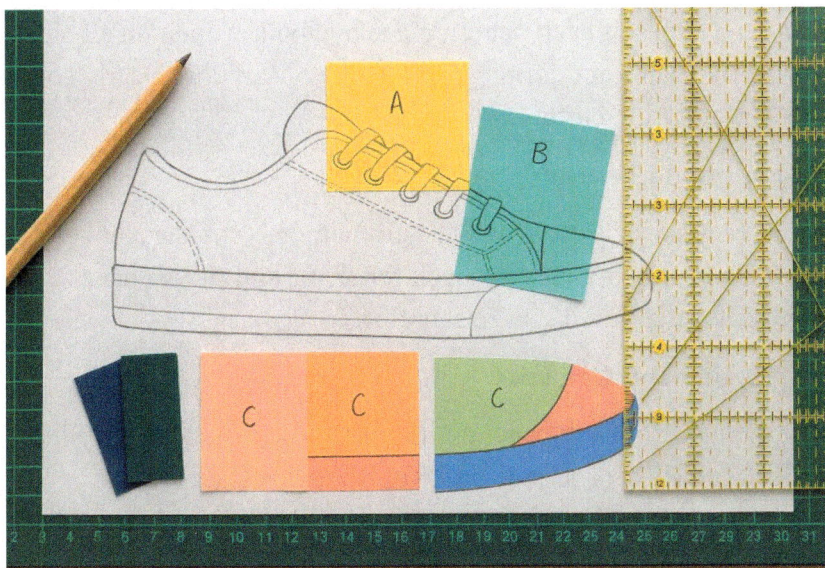

Create custom quilt templates by breaking your sneaker's shape into stitchable sections.

A. Step-by-Step Lesson: Make Your Custom Quilt Patterns

1. Gather Your Pattern-Making Supplies

You'll need plain paper (printer paper, tracing paper, or even cardstock), pencil, ruler, scissors, and your sneaker measurements from Day 10.

2. Draw the Basic Shapes

Using your measurements, draw the shape of each sneaker panel— side, toe box, tongue, heel, etc.—onto the paper. For curved sections, sketch gently and adjust the shape as needed until it matches the sneaker's contour.

3. Add Seam Allowance

Extend the edges of each pattern piece by about ¼ inch on all sides to allow for seams and turning under edges. Mark this clearly so you don't forget during cutting.

4. Cut and Test the Templates

Cut out each paper pattern and test-fit them on your sneaker base. Tape them lightly in place to check for shape and fit. Adjust as needed and re-cut until you're satisfied.

5. Label and Organize

Write the name of each panel on its pattern piece (e.g., "Left Side Panel," "Toe Box") and indicate "Top" and "Outside" for orientation. Keep all your patterns in an envelope or folder for easy access.

B. Why This Matters

Accurate patterns ensure your fabric fits the shape of your sneaker perfectly. Without templates, you risk wasting fabric or ending up with mismatched panels. A little time spent drafting now will save time and frustration later when you begin cutting and sewing.

C. Tips & Creative Ideas

- **Use Cardstock for Longevity**: Thicker paper holds up better if you plan to reuse your pattern.

- **Color-Code Pieces**: Highlight different sections for easy reference during cutting.

- **Keep a Master Sheet**: Tape mini versions of your patterns to a notebook page for quick reference.

- **Try a Mock-Up**: Make a rough test using scrap fabric to check how pieces wrap around the shoe.

Today you created the custom puzzle pieces that will shape your entire project. These quilt patterns are the key to making your sneakers not only stylish but also well-fitted and functional. Tomorrow, you'll bring them to life by cutting and prepping your actual fabrics. Your vision is coming together—piece by piece.

Day 12: Precisely Cut and Prep Your Quilt Fabrics

Today marks the exciting transition from planning to hands-on making. With your custom quilt patterns complete, it's time to cut your chosen fabrics with care and precision. This step sets the tone for the rest of your project, so accuracy and organization are key.

By the end of today, you'll have all your fabric pieces cut, labeled, and ready to quilt, assemble, and attach to your sneaker base in the coming days.

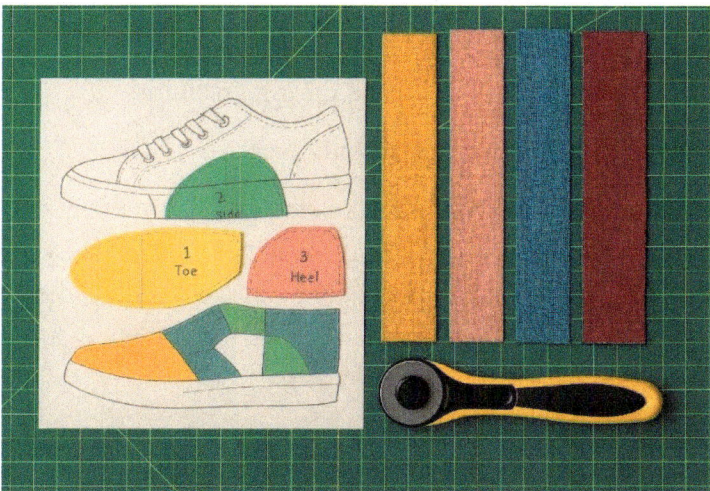

Use pattern templates to cut fabric precisely, keeping your designs symmetrical and clean.

A. Step-by-Step Lesson: Cut and Prep Your Fabric Panels

1. Organize Your Workspace

Lay out your fabrics, tools, and pattern pieces. Use a clean, flat surface with plenty of space to move and rotate materials. A cutting mat is ideal for clean, straight lines.

2. Pin or Trace Your Patterns

Place each paper pattern onto the fabric and pin it securely in place, or trace around it using a fabric-safe marking tool. Make sure your fabric is smoothed out and wrinkle-free before tracing or cutting.

3. Cut Carefully and Consistently

Use sharp fabric scissors or a rotary cutter to cut each piece as cleanly as possible. Follow the seam allowance lines if you added them on Day 11. Double-check each piece after cutting to ensure it matches your pattern.

4. Group and Label Each Section

Separate the cut pieces by sneaker section—side panels, toe boxes, tongues, heels, etc. Use sticky notes, small bags, or index cards to label each group for easy reference during assembly.

5. Prep for Quilting (Optional)

If you plan to pre-quilt your panels before attaching them, cut matching pieces of low-loft batting or interfacing now. Layer them with the fabric pieces so you're ready to start quilting in the next steps.

B. Why This Matters

Clean, accurate fabric cuts lead to smooth quilting, tight seams, and a professional finish. Taking time to prep your materials properly also helps prevent mistakes, saves fabric, and makes the rest of the process more enjoyable and efficient.

C. Tips & Creative Ideas

- **Stack & Cut Duplicates**: Cut mirrored left/right panels at once by folding fabric in half.

- **Press Fabrics First**: Iron fabrics before cutting to remove wrinkles and improve accuracy.

- **Use a Color Code**: Keep similar fabrics together by color to avoid mix-ups during assembly.

- **Create a Cutting Checklist**: Cross off each panel as you complete it.

D. Reflection & Motivation

Today you've officially begun the physical creation of your quilted sneakers. Each piece you've cut represents a part of your vision coming to life. With your fabrics ready to go, you're fully equipped to begin the quilting process. Tomorrow, you'll learn essential stitches that bring texture, strength, and personality to your project. Let's keep building!

Chapter 4 Review: L – Layout & Pattern Preparation

Chapter 4 covered **Days 10–12** of your journey through the 50-Day **Q-U-I-L-T-I-N-G S-N-E-A-K-E-R-S** system, focusing on **L – Layout & Pattern Preparation**. This chapter turned your design from concept into reality by guiding you through the measuring, drafting, and fabric preparation stages—laying the technical groundwork needed to bring your quilted sneaker panels to life.

Day 10 – Measure Your Sneaker Base Accurately

- **Understand the sneaker anatomy** – Learn the key areas where quilted panels will be applied: toe box, sides, heel, and tongue.

- **Use the right tools** – Rulers, flexible measuring tape, and marking pens ensure precision.

- **Record measurements clearly** – Take accurate notes of each section to guide pattern creation.

- **Prepare for symmetry** – Consistent measurements lead to balanced, professional-looking designs.

Day 11 – Draft & Create Sneaker Quilt Patterns

- **Transfer measurements to paper** – Use your Day 10 data to draw each sneaker panel as a flat pattern piece.

- **Label and organize patterns** – Mark pattern names, seam allowances, and orientation for each section.

- **Test your pattern fit** – Use scrap paper or muslin to test your pattern against the sneaker shape.

- **Refine for accuracy** – Adjust curves and corners to ensure clean panel placement when quilting and attaching.

Day 12 – Precisely Cut and Prep Your Quilt Fabrics

- **Use your patterns to cut fabric** – Pin or trace your pattern pieces onto your chosen fabrics.

- **Cut with accuracy** – Use sharp scissors or a rotary cutter on a self-healing mat for clean edges.

- **Organize your fabric pieces** – Group panels by sneaker zone to streamline your workflow.

- **Stabilize and prep** – Add interfacing or batting as needed to support stitching and structure.

By the end of Chapter 4, your quilted sneaker design has gone from sketch to physical parts, prepped and ready for assembly. In **Chapter 5: T – Techniques for Quilting Sneakers (Days 13–15)**, you'll learn the essential stitching techniques and design methods to bring texture, pattern, and life to your custom panels. The making begins now.

Chapter 5: T – Techniques for Quilting Sneakers

Chapter 5 highlights **T**—which stands for **Techniques**—in the **50-day Q-U-I-L-T-I-N.G S-N-E-A-K-E.R.S System**. In this chapter, you'll master the skills needed to bring your quilted sneakers to life with precision and style. On **Day 13**, you'll dive into essential quilting stitches, learning the foundational techniques that will support your designs. **Day 14** will expand your skillset as you explore diamond, grid, and geometric designs, adding unique patterns to your sneakers. Finally, **Day 15** introduces more advanced sneaker quilting methods, challenging you to refine your craft and push creative boundaries. This chapter provides the techniques and know-how to elevate your quilting skills, ensuring your sneaker designs are both beautiful and durable.

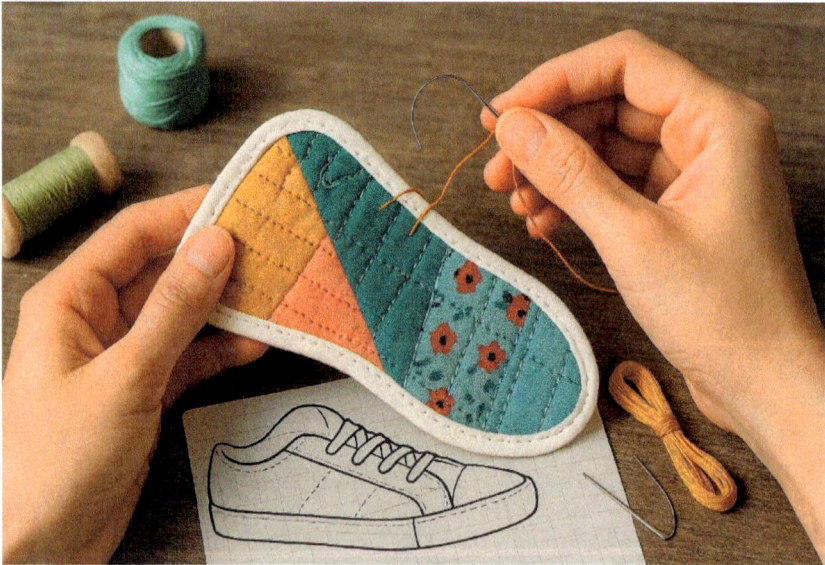

Master foundational quilting techniques before stitching directly onto your sneaker project.

Day 13: Learn Essential Quilting Stitches

Today, you'll learn the foundational stitches that bring your quilt panels to life. Whether you plan to hand-stitch or use a sewing machine, understanding a few key techniques will help you create secure, stylish, and well-crafted quilted sneaker panels.

Stitching isn't just about function—it's also a design tool. The way you stitch can add texture, enhance your patterns, and define your style. Today's focus is mastering the basics so you can confidently quilt your fabric pieces in the coming days.

Build your stitch library with reliable techniques suited for tight curves and fabric layering.

A. Step-by-Step Lesson: Practice Essential Stitches

1. Running Stitch

This is the most basic hand-sewing stitch. Pass your needle in and out of the fabric in a straight line, creating evenly spaced dashes. Great for securing layers or outlining shapes.

2. Backstitch

Ideal for stronger seams, the backstitch fills in the gaps of a running stitch. After one forward stitch, bring the needle up ahead, then go back into the previous hole. Use this for areas needing extra hold.

3. Straight-Line Machine Stitching

If using a sewing machine, practice stitching in straight lines. Use a walking foot if available—it helps feed multiple layers evenly. Start slow and guide your quilt sandwich carefully through the machine.

4. Echo Stitching

This technique involves stitching lines that "echo" around a shape, adding texture and dimension. Use this for decorative effects or to emphasize geometric designs.

5. Basting Stitch (Optional)

For temporarily holding layers together before permanent stitching, use long, loose stitches called basting. You can do this by hand or with a long stitch setting on your machine.

B. Why This Matters

Mastering essential stitches gives you the skill and control to bring your panels together cleanly and confidently. These stitches form the backbone of your quilted designs and ensure they hold up to wear and movement once attached to the sneaker.

C. Tips & Creative Ideas

- **Use Contrasting Thread**: Make stitches stand out as a design element.

- **Practice on Scraps**: Try different stitches on leftover fabric before quilting your panels.

- **Mark Stitch Lines**: Lightly draw guide lines on fabric with chalk or fabric pen.

- **Try Decorative Stitches**: If your machine has special stitch settings, experiment with them on your test fabric.

D. Reflection & Motivation

Today, you took a major step toward becoming a confident quilted sneaker maker. Stitching transforms flat fabric into something textured, dynamic, and full of character. With your basic techniques mastered, tomorrow you'll start applying those stitches to create bold quilt patterns that define your sneaker's style. You're stitching your vision into reality—one line at a time.

Day 14: Quilt Diamond, Grid, & Geometric Designs

Today's focus is on bringing structure and visual impact to your quilt panels using clean, eye-catching patterns. Diamond, grid, and geometric quilting designs are timeless, versatile, and ideal for sneaker panels because they add texture without overwhelming small areas.

You'll learn how to plan and stitch these patterns on your fabric panels using the techniques you practiced yesterday. These designs will elevate your sneakers from simple to stunning—adding definition and a modern touch to your creative layout.

Experiment with pattern symmetry and thread tension before applying to your sneaker canvas.

A. Step-by-Step Lesson: Quilt Bold, Structured Designs

1. Prepare Your Fabric "Sandwich"

Layer your quilt panel: backing fabric (wrong side down), batting or interfacing, and top fabric (right side up). Secure the layers with pins or clips to prevent shifting during stitching.

2. Mark Your Design Lines

Use a ruler and fabric-safe marking tool to draw your pattern onto the top fabric.

- **Grid**: Draw evenly spaced horizontal and vertical lines for a checkerboard effect.

- **Diamond**: Create diagonal lines in both directions for a crisscrossed diamond pattern.

o **Geometric**: Experiment with triangles, hexagons, or offset blocks—just keep the shapes clean and symmetrical.

3. Start Stitching

Use a running stitch (by hand) or straight stitch (by machine) to follow your marked lines. Work from the center outward to minimize fabric shifting and puckering.

4. Maintain Even Spacing

Keep stitch lines consistent, spacing lines ½ inch to 1 inch apart depending on your desired texture. Take your time—precision here gives your panels a polished, professional finish.

5. Trim and Press the Panels

Once stitching is complete, trim any excess batting and gently press the quilted fabric with an iron to smooth it out and flatten seams.

B. Why This Matters

Grid and geometric quilting patterns add structure, strength, and style to your panels. They make the fabric easier to handle and give each sneaker section a bold, modern texture. These classic designs are a go-to foundation for almost any sneaker quilting project.

C. Tips & Creative Ideas

- **Mix Patterns**: Use grid on the side panel, diamonds on the tongue, and triangles on the heel for variety.

- **Go Bold with Thread**: Try a contrasting thread color to make your quilting lines pop.

- **Mini Blocks**: Shrink geometric shapes to fit smaller areas like the toe box or collar.

- **Layer Designs**: Add echo stitching or borders around your quilt blocks for extra flair.

D. Reflection & Motivation

Today, you transformed fabric into dimension and design. Quilting geometric patterns is where creativity meets structure—and it sets the tone for the rest of your sneaker build. Tomorrow, you'll explore advanced quilting methods to add even more depth and artistic flair to your panels. Your skills are growing, and your project is leveling up fast!

Day 15: Explore Advanced Sneaker Quilting Methods

Now that you've mastered essential stitches and geometric quilting, it's time to level up. Today, you'll explore advanced quilting methods that add texture, complexity, and artistic impact to your sneaker panels. These techniques give your work a signature style— making your sneakers look more like high-end, handcrafted art pieces.

Don't worry if you're still getting comfortable with quilting. These methods are optional and adaptable. Use what excites you, and save the rest for future projects as your confidence grows.

Advanced techniques add texture and depth—ideal for standout sneaker projects.

A. Step-by-Step Lesson: Try Advanced Quilting Techniques

1. Trapunto (Raised Quilting)

Add extra dimension by stitching around a shape, then stuffing it slightly from behind with batting or fiberfill. This creates a puffy, sculpted look—great for initials, logos, or small icons.

2. Appliqué Accents

Cut shapes (stars, letters, symbols, or designs) from fabric and stitch them onto your quilted panel. Use a zigzag or blanket stitch around the edges to secure and decorate. This adds a layered, textured look to your design.

3. Free-Motion Quilting

With a free-motion foot on your sewing machine, guide the fabric manually to create swirling lines, curves, or custom artwork. This technique takes practice but offers limitless design potential.

4. Quilted Embroidery Combos

Combine quilting stitches with hand embroidery. Add outlines, stitched motifs, or borders on top of your quilted blocks. This creates a dynamic mix of texture and detail.

5. Reverse Quilting

Use negative space as a design element. Quilt around shapes and leave them unstitched to let the pattern "pop" from the background. Works well with bold blocks or statement icons.

B. Why This Matters

Advanced quilting gives your sneaker panels that next-level "wow" factor. These techniques allow you to tell a story, express your personality, or simply add artistic flair. When done right, they set your work apart and push your creative boundaries.

C. Tips & Creative Ideas

- **Start Small**: Try one advanced method on a small panel, like the tongue or heel.

- **Sketch First**: Map out any free-motion or appliqué designs before stitching.

- **Use Stabilizer**: For intricate stitching, add stabilizer under your panel for support.

- **Mix with Basics**: Don't overload—combine one advanced element with simple quilting for balance.

D. Reflection & Motivation

Today, you expanded your creative toolbox and learned how to add custom flair to your sneaker panels. Whether you tried one advanced method or explored them all, you're growing into a true quilted sneaker designer. Next up: transforming your finished panels into wearable art as you begin assembling them onto your sneakers. You're doing incredible—keep going strong!

Chapter 5 Review: T – Techniques for Quilting Sneakers

Chapter 5 covered **Days 13–15** of your journey through the 50-Day **Q-U-I-L-T-I-N-G S-N-E-A-K-E-R-S** system, focusing on **T – Techniques for Quilting Sneakers**. This chapter brought your materials and design to life with texture, movement, and detail. You practiced foundational stitches, explored classic quilting motifs, and tested out advanced methods to elevate your work.

Day 13 – Learn Essential Quilting Stitches

- **Master basic quilting techniques** – Learn straight stitches, running stitches, and backstitching by hand or machine.

- **Explore stitch function and form** – Understand how stitching strengthens panels and adds decorative texture.

- **Practice control and spacing** – Keep stitches even and aligned to ensure durability and visual appeal.

- **Build stitching confidence** – Get comfortable stitching on layered fabric with batting or interfacing.

Day 14 – Quilt Diamond, Grid, & Geometric Designs

- **Apply structured patterns** – Learn how to quilt diamonds, squares, grids, and chevrons for modern, eye-catching effects.

- **Mark your guides** – Use chalk, erasable pens, or templates to keep lines consistent across panels.

- **Balance bold vs. subtle** – Use thread color and stitch density to control how much your pattern stands out.

- **Adapt designs to sneaker zones** – Fit your geometric layout to the shape and size of each panel.

Day 15 – Explore Advanced Sneaker Quilting Methods

- **Experiment with dimensional techniques** – Try trapunto, echo quilting, or layered effects to add depth.

- **Incorporate curved or free-motion stitching** – Add flow and organic texture to break up rigid shapes.

- **Mix quilting with embroidery** – Introduce flourishes, monograms, or signature details to customize your work.

- **Refine your skill set** – Focus on precision, planning, and creativity to elevate your craftsmanship.

By the end of Chapter 5, you've mastered essential and advanced quilting techniques that turn your fabric panels into expressive, stitched works of art. In **Chapter 6: I – Integrate Quilted Panels onto Sneakers (Days 16–18)**, you'll move from prepping to assembling—learning how to secure your quilted panels onto the sneaker base with professional-quality finishing.

Chapter 6: I – Integrate Quilted Panels onto Sneakers

Chapter 6 focuses on **I**—which stands for **Integrate**—in the **50-day Q-U-I-L-T-I-N-G S-N-E-A-K-E.R.S System**. In this chapter, you'll learn how to seamlessly incorporate your quilted panels into your sneakers for a polished, professional look. On **Day 16**, you'll begin by creating and preparing your quilted panels, ensuring they're ready for integration into your design. On **Day 17**, you'll move on to securing these panels onto your sneakers, with detailed instructions on how to align and stitch them for a perfect fit. Finally, **Day 18** will guide you through perfecting your stitching and assembly techniques, helping you achieve smooth, even results. This chapter equips you with the tools and skills necessary to bring your quilted panels to life and turn your sneakers into wearable art.

Seamlessly merge your quilting work onto real sneakers with clean integration and steady assembly.

Day 16: Create & Prepare Quilted Panels

Today marks the transition from standalone fabric work to building your wearable art. With your fabrics cut and quilting designs stitched, it's time to assemble your quilted panels—structured pieces that will fit and form to your sneakers. These panels are the heart of your custom sneaker design, and today you'll prepare them for attachment.

You'll shape, trim, and prep each panel so they're clean, uniform, and ready to be applied to your sneaker base in the coming days.

Pre-quilted panels allow you to control design and detail before committing to your sneakers.

A. Step-by-Step Lesson: Assemble and Prep Your Panels

1. Gather Your Finished Quilted Pieces

Lay out all your quilted sections—sides, toe box, tongue, heel, and any extras. Match each piece to its corresponding sneaker section and confirm sizes using your paper patterns from earlier.

2. Trim Excess Layers

Trim the edges of each panel neatly, especially if any batting or backing fabric extends beyond the stitched lines. Keep the shape clean and consistent with your original pattern.

3. Shape the Panels for Fit

Gently curve or fold each panel to mimic the natural contour of the sneaker. This helps soften the fabric and ensures better alignment during assembly.

4. Add Edge Finishes (Optional)

If you want a polished look or plan to leave edges exposed, finish them with a zigzag stitch, bias tape, or a folded fabric edge. This step helps prevent fraying and adds a professional touch.

5. Label and Organize

Keep each panel grouped and labeled by left/right and sneaker section. Having everything clearly sorted will make the next steps more efficient.

B. Why This Matters

Creating structured panels is the final preparation before attachment. Well-shaped, prepped quilt panels allow for smooth application, clean seams, and a comfortable fit on the sneaker. This step ensures that your hard design and quilting work transitions cleanly into the final wearable piece.

C. Tips & Creative Ideas

- **Steam Press Panels**: A gentle press can help set curves and remove wrinkles.
- **Test Fit with Tape**: Lightly tape panels to your sneaker to preview placement.

- **Edge Sealant**: Use fabric glue on raw edges if you're not finishing them with stitching.

- **Reinforce Corners**: Add an extra layer of stitching to points or curves that may experience stress.

D. Reflection & Motivation

Today you brought all your quilting work together into beautifully crafted panels. With everything trimmed, shaped, and ready, you're fully prepped for the most exciting part—attaching your work to the sneakers themselves. Tomorrow, you'll secure your panels with precision, care, and creativity. You're getting closer to the finish line, one stitch at a time.

Day 17: Secure Quilted Panels onto Sneakers

Today's the day you start transforming your quilted pieces into wearable art by attaching them to your sneaker base. This step brings together everything you've worked on so far—design, stitching, shaping—and applies it directly to your shoes. It's a hands-on process that requires patience, precision, and a little creativity.

You'll choose between stitching, gluing, or a combination of both, depending on your materials and comfort level. The goal is to securely attach each panel in a way that fits well, feels comfortable, and looks professional.

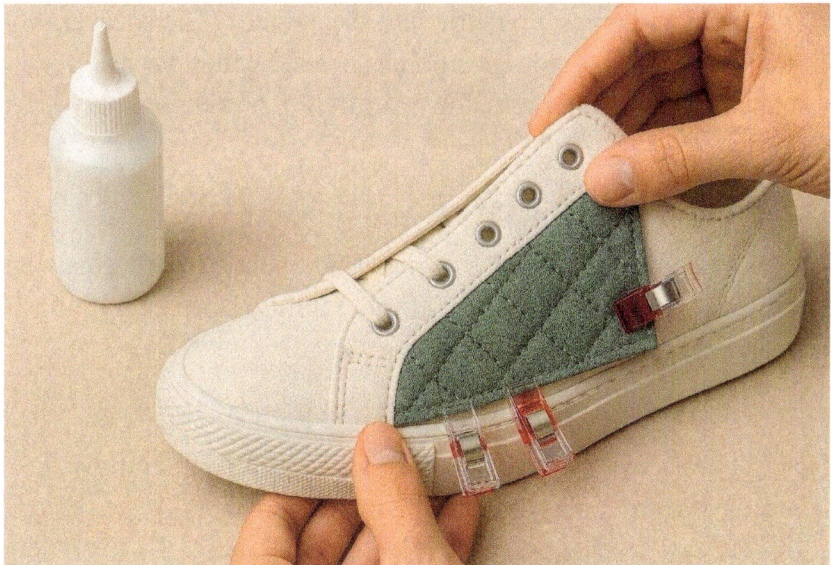

Carefully align panels before stitching to maintain design symmetry and shoe flexibility.

A. Step-by-Step Lesson: Attach Panels with Confidence

1. **Choose Your Attachment Method**

   - **Sewing**: Best for canvas sneakers and thin panels. Use a curved or upholstery needle and strong thread.

   - **Fabric or Shoe Glue**: Ideal for thick panels, curved areas, or where sewing is difficult. Use a strong adhesive like E6000 or Shoe Goo.

   - **Hybrid**: Use glue to hold panels in place, then reinforce with stitching for strength and style.

2. **Apply One Panel at a Time**

Start with the side panels, then move to toe box, tongue, heel, and collar. This order helps keep your design aligned and balanced. Use clips or pins to hold each panel temporarily in place.

3. **Smooth and Shape as You Go**

Work slowly and press the fabric into the curves of the sneaker. Smooth out wrinkles and reposition as needed before securing permanently. If gluing, press down firmly for 30–60 seconds per section.

4. Reinforce Key Areas

Corners, edges, and high-stress points (like the toe or heel) may need extra glue or a few added stitches for durability. Keep everything clean and neat for a polished look.

5. Let It Set

If using glue, let your sneakers sit for at least 24 hours to fully dry and cure before wearing or handling them too much.

B. Why This Matters

This is the step that turns your quilted panels into finished, functional footwear. Attaching the fabric correctly ensures your sneakers are secure, comfortable, and long-lasting. A clean, careful application also gives your shoes a high-quality finish that reflects the effort you've put into every detail.

C. Tips & Creative Ideas

- **Use a Thimble**: Hand-stitching through sneakers can be tough—protect your fingers.

- **Work in Layers**: Attach base panels first, then add accents or overlays later.

- **Clean Edges**: Trim or tuck any uneven fabric edges before final sealing.

- **Keep a Damp Cloth Nearby**: Wipe away any excess glue before it dries.

D. Reflection & Motivation

You've just completed one of the most rewarding steps in your quilted sneaker journey—watching your designs become real, wearable pieces. Tomorrow, we'll focus on perfecting your stitching and finishing techniques to make sure your sneakers are as strong and stylish as they are unique. You're almost there—keep it up!

Day 18: Perfect Stitching & Assembly Techniques

Now that your quilted panels are attached, today is about refining the details. This step focuses on clean stitching, secure assembly, and making sure your sneakers are comfortable, durable, and polished. Perfecting these techniques adds the final layer of professionalism to your design.

Even small adjustments can make a big difference. Whether you're reinforcing seams, smoothing edges, or adding finishing stitches, today's work ensures your quilted sneakers are both beautiful and built to last.

Use reinforced stitches and hand alignment techniques to secure your work without puckering.

A. Step-by-Step Lesson: Refine Your Stitching and Assembly

1. Inspect All Seams and Edges

Look over each panel to check for loose threads, uneven fabric, or lifted edges. Identify areas that need reinforcement, trimming, or touch-up stitching.

2. Reinforce Stitch Lines

Go over any essential seams—especially on the toe, heel, or side panels—with a backstitch (hand) or a second line of straight stitching (machine). This adds strength in areas that will flex or rub during wear.

3. Tidy Up Edges

Tuck in or trim excess fabric where needed. Use a whipstitch or blanket stitch to finish raw edges if they're exposed, or carefully seal them with fabric glue for a smooth look.

4. Secure Overlays and Accents

If you've added extra layers like patches, appliqués, or embroidery, now's the time to double-check their attachment. Stitch or glue them securely to avoid lifting with use.

5. Test Fit and Flexibility

Gently wear or bend the sneakers to make sure the panels move with the shoe and don't restrict comfort. Adjust stitching or trim bulk if necessary for a better fit.

B. Why This Matters

This final stage of assembly turns your sneakers from a handmade craft into a wearable product. Clean stitching, reinforced seams, and smooth edges show your attention to detail and make your sneakers durable and comfortable for real-world use.

C. Tips & Creative Ideas

- **Match Thread Colors**: Use color-matched thread for invisible reinforcement or bold colors for contrast stitching.

- **Add Decorative Stitching**: Create borders or outlines for a custom finish.

- **Use Pliers or Thimbles**: Helpful when stitching through thick areas or tough sneaker fabric.

- **Finish with Fabric Sealant**: Dab edges with fray check or a thin line of glue for added hold.

D. Reflection & Motivation

Today, you perfected the craftsmanship that brings your quilted sneakers to life. These finishing touches are what take your design from DIY to designer-quality. Next, you'll explore creative ways to customize and embellish your sneakers—adding the details that make them unmistakably yours. You're doing incredible work—this is what artistry looks like in motion.

Chapter 6 Review: I – Integrate Quilted Panels onto Sneakers

Chapter 6 covered **Days 16–18** of your journey through the 50-Day **Q-U-I-L-T-I-N-G S-N-E-A-K-E-R-S** system, focusing on **I – Integrate Quilted Panels onto Sneakers**. This chapter guided you through the essential transition from finished quilted panels to fully assembled sneakers. You learned how to construct, attach, and fine-tune each component for structure, comfort, and style.

Day 16 – Create & Prepare Quilted Panels

- **Assemble your quilt layers** – Combine fabric, batting, and backing with your selected stitching technique.

- **Quilt and shape each panel** – Add texture and definition using your chosen patterns and thread.

- **Trim and finish edges** – Clean up your panel shapes to ensure they match your sneaker templates.

- **Prep for attachment** – Press panels flat, reinforce weak areas, and organize panels by sneaker zone.

Day 17 – Secure Quilted Panels onto Sneakers

- **Choose your attachment method** – Use strong adhesives, hand-stitching, or a combination depending on the sneaker and panel.

- **Apply panels carefully** – Align each piece before securing, smoothing as you go for a wrinkle-free finish.

- **Anchor edges for durability** – Stitch or reinforce seams to prevent peeling or fraying over time.

- **Check for balance** – Ensure both shoes are symmetrical in placement, spacing, and overall feel.

Day 18 – Perfect Stitching & Assembly Techniques

- **Reinforce high-stress areas** – Use extra stitching around corners, heels, and the toe box for long-term wear.

- **Add topstitching or edge finishes** – Enhance detail and durability with clean stitching around borders.

- **Smooth transitions between materials** – Blend quilted sections with the original sneaker surface using flexible adhesives or stitching.

- **Inspect overall structure** – Ensure comfort, stability, and style are all in place before calling your sneakers complete.

By the end of Chapter 6, you've gone from raw panels to a fully assembled pair of quilted sneakers—crafted with precision, personality, and professional finish. In **Chapter 7: N – Navigate Customizing & Detailing (Days 19–21)**, you'll take your sneakers to the next level with embroidery, embellishments, and creative mixed-media additions.

Chapter 7: N – Navigate Customizing & Detailing

Chapter 7 focuses on **N**—which stands for **Navigate**—in the **50-day Q-U-I-L-T-I-N-G S-N-E-A-K-E-R.S System**. This chapter dives into the exciting world of customizing and detailing your quilted sneakers to make them truly unique. On **Day 19**, you'll learn how to add intricate embroidery and decorative quilting to your sneakers, transforming them into stunning, personalized works of art. On **Day 20**, you'll explore how to enhance your designs with embellishments such as beads, patches, and trims, adding texture and flair to your project. Finally, **Day 21** introduces you to mixed media techniques, where you'll combine quilting with other materials like leather, fabric paints, and appliqué for a bold, multi-dimensional finish. This chapter empowers you to inject creativity and individuality into every pair of sneakers, ensuring they stand out as one-of-a-kind pieces.

Add creative flair with custom details that reflect your personal style.

Day 19: Add Embroidery & Decorative Quilting

Today's focus is all about adding flair, personality, and artistry through embroidery and decorative quilting. These finishing touches give your sneakers a signature style—whether it's subtle, bold, or full of creative expression. Now that your panels are attached and secured, you can start layering in unique details that truly make your sneakers one of a kind.

Decorative stitching is where function meets flair. It adds texture, color, and storytelling to your design—transforming your quilted sneakers into wearable works of art.

Embroidery adds texture and personality to your quilted sneaker canvas.

A. Step-by-Step Lesson: Stitch in the Details

1. **Choose Your Style and Motifs**

Decide what kind of embroidery or decorative quilting fits your theme. Common motifs include initials, symbols, stars, flowers, geometric shapes, or simple lines and borders. Keep scale in mind—smaller, tighter designs work best on limited sneaker space.

2. Mark Your Designs First

Lightly draw or trace your design onto the quilted panel using a washable fabric pen or tailor's chalk. This helps guide your stitches and maintain clean lines.

3. Select Your Threads and Needles

Use embroidery floss or colorful thread that contrasts or complements your panel colors. Choose a sharp embroidery or crewel needle suited for layered fabric.

4. Apply Embroidery by Hand

Use simple stitches like backstitch, satin stitch, chain stitch, or French knots. Start small—embellish one panel at a time and step back to see how it enhances the overall design.

5. Decorative Quilting Lines

Beyond embroidery, you can quilt designs directly into your panels: echo around a motif, outline shapes, or stitch patterns like waves, loops, or borders. These stitches add structure and style at the same time.

B. Why This Matters

Embroidery and decorative quilting give your sneakers that personal, handmade edge. These embellishments make your work stand out and reflect your personality. They also add texture, depth, and visual interest to each panel—making your sneakers feel finished and expressive.

C. Tips & Creative Ideas

- **Use Metallic or Glow-in-the-Dark Thread**: Add an unexpected twist.

- **Stitch Around Edges**: Frame your panels with decorative borders or dotted lines.

- **Embroider a Message**: Add initials, quotes, or a word that inspires you.

- **Test on Scrap First**: Practice the design and spacing before stitching your actual panel.

D. Reflection & Motivation

Today you stitched in your story, one thread at a time. Embroidery and decorative quilting allow your voice and vision to shine through in subtle or striking ways. Tomorrow, you'll take it even further with embellishments and unique details that add character, sparkle, and edge to your custom kicks. You're officially in the detail stage— enjoy every creative second!

Day 20: Embellishments & Unique Sneaker Details

Now that your quilted panels and embroidery are complete, it's time to turn your sneakers into statement pieces. Today is all about adding embellishments and unique details—finishing touches that highlight your creativity and make your sneakers unforgettable.

Whether you want subtle flair or bold personality, there are countless ways to personalize your shoes even further. From laces to hardware, every detail is an opportunity to express your style and bring your design to life.

Use embellishments to make your sneakers pop with eye-catching finishes.

A. Step-by-Step Lesson: Add Personalized Embellishments

1. Explore Your Options

Choose embellishments that align with your aesthetic. Options include iron-on patches, buttons, beads, studs, sequins, lace trims, or even fabric paint. Think about where and how they'll enhance your design without overpowering it.

2. Plan Placement Carefully

Lay your embellishments on the sneaker to test positioning. Focus on accent areas like the tongue, side panels, or near the laces. Use symmetry or asymmetry depending on your style goals.

3. Attach with Precision

- o **For sew-on elements**: Use a strong needle and reinforced stitching.

o **For glue-on items**: Use fabric glue or strong adhesive and press firmly. Let it dry completely before moving the sneaker.

o **For iron-ons**: Follow the manufacturer's instructions, and use a pressing cloth to protect the fabric.

4. **Customize Laces and Eyelets**

Swap standard laces for ribbon, leather, or patterned shoelaces. You can also paint or embellish the eyelets with studs, gems, or metallic markers for added flair.

5. **Add Interior or Hidden Details**

Want to personalize even further? Embroider or paint a message inside the tongue, around the ankle lining, or under the insole for a secret, special touch.

B. Why This Matters

Embellishments add polish, depth, and originality. They take your sneakers from "customized" to "completely yours." These small design choices are what turn your work into something that people notice, remember, and admire. It's your chance to finish strong and fully own your artistic voice.

C. Tips & Creative Ideas

- **Go 3D**: Layer embellishments over quilting for added texture.

- **Use Theme Inspiration**: Match embellishments to your board—retro, sporty, minimalist, maximalist, etc.

- **Limit Overcrowding**: Leave space for your quilting and fabrics to breathe.

- **Create a Signature Detail**: A unique design element you can repeat on future pairs.

D. Reflection & Motivation

Today, you added the final visual elements that give your quilted sneakers attitude and identity. These creative flourishes reflect your imagination, attention to detail, and personal taste. Tomorrow, we'll take customization even further by exploring mixed media techniques to blend textures and materials for a bold, innovative finish. Keep creating—you're building something amazing!

Day 21: Mixed Media Quilted Sneaker Techniques

Today you'll push the boundaries of traditional quilting by incorporating mixed media techniques into your sneaker design. Mixed media means combining different materials—like leather, mesh, vinyl, felt, metal, or paint—with your quilted fabric to add depth, contrast, and originality.

This is your chance to experiment, break the rules, and give your sneakers a unique visual and tactile personality. The result? A custom creation that blends craft, fashion, and art.

Combine materials and techniques to create bold, mixed-media sneaker statements.

A. Step-by-Step Lesson: Blend Materials Like a Designer

1. Gather Mixed Media Materials

Pull together a variety of elements you'd like to experiment with: metallic fabric, faux leather, mesh, denim, felt, sheer overlays, chains, zippers, or even recycled materials like old jewelry or keychains.

2. Choose Accent Zones

Select specific areas to apply your mixed media elements—like the heel tab, lace panel, tongue, or outer side panel. Let your quilted fabric remain the base while the mixed media adds dimension.

3. Test Material Flexibility

Make sure any material you use can bend, curve, and move with the sneaker. Thicker pieces should be trimmed or softened with heat or fabric softener to prevent stiffness or discomfort.

4. Layer with Intention

Combine soft and firm textures, shiny and matte surfaces, or opaque and sheer layers to create contrast. Use stitching, adhesive, or rivets to attach depending on the material type.

5. Seal, Stitch, or Reinforce

Use a strong stitch (hand or machine), E6000 glue, or double-sided fusible interfacing for layered applications. Test how each material holds up when worn—comfort and durability matter just as much as looks.

B. Why This Matters

Mixed media techniques take your creativity to new heights. By blending unexpected materials with quilting, you create one-of-a-kind sneakers that reflect innovation, craftsmanship, and a fearless approach to design. It also opens the door for future exploration and evolving your style.

C. Tips & Creative Ideas

- **Add Clear Vinyl Windows**: Reveal underlying quilt designs or place messages underneath.

- **Layer Mesh or Netting**: Overlay a section of quilting for a sporty or modern look.

- **Try Leather Accents**: Add luxury by using faux or real leather around the toe or heel.

- **Use Found Objects**: Repurpose charms, zipper pulls, or broken jewelry for unique details.

D. Reflection & Motivation

You've officially stepped into the world of wearable art. Today's work represents freedom, experimentation, and advanced creativity. With quilting as your foundation, you've expanded into custom design territory—creating something truly bold, personal, and expressive. Tomorrow, we'll move into finishing techniques to polish and protect your masterpiece. You're doing incredible work—keep the energy flowing!

Chapter 7 Review: N – Navigate Customizing & Detailing

Chapter 7 covered **Days 19–21** of your journey through the 50-Day **Q-U-I-L-T-I-N-G S-N-E-A-K-E-R-S** system, focusing on **N – Navigate Customizing & Detailing**. This chapter was all about adding artistry and personality to your quilted sneakers through embroidery, embellishments, and experimental mixed media. These finishing touches transform your sneakers from handmade to one-of-a-kind statement pieces.

Day 19 – Add Embroidery & Decorative Quilting

- **Stitch visual interest into your panels** – Use embroidery floss, decorative thread, or metallic accents.

- **Add patterns, symbols, or text** – Stitch meaningful motifs, names, dates, or shapes that tell a story.

- **Balance detail with structure** – Enhance without overwhelming—make sure stitching supports your design.

- **Customize each pair** – Use embroidery to give every sneaker a signature, hand-touched look.

Day 20 – Embellishments & Unique Sneaker Details

- **Add texture and sparkle** – Incorporate patches, beads, sequins, buttons, rivets, or fabric paints.

- **Highlight key zones** – Focus embellishments on areas like the heel, tongue, or laces for maximum effect.

- **Ensure security and durability** – Reinforce embellishments so they stay intact during wear.

- **Create signature styling cues** – Develop a recognizable look or detail that sets your work apart.

Day 21 – Mixed Media Quilted Sneaker Techniques

- **Combine materials for bold results** – Blend fabric with leather, mesh, vinyl, rope, or unconventional textiles.

- **Layer thoughtfully** – Use overlays, cut-outs, or fabric fusion for dynamic texture and contrast.

- **Experiment with advanced tools** – Try fabric burning, heat-press vinyl, or laser-cut accents for next-level effects.

- **Keep wearability in mind** – Prioritize comfort and mobility while pushing creative boundaries.

By the end of Chapter 7, you've developed a unique creative voice through detail and decoration. Your quilted sneakers now reflect not only technical skill but deep personal style. In **Chapter 8: G – Guarantee Professional-Level Finishing (Days 22–24)**, you'll shift focus to refining edges, protecting your work, and completing quality checks for a polished, long-lasting final product.

Chapter 8: G – Guarantee Professional-Level Finishing

Chapter 8 is all about **G**, which stands for **Guarantee** in the **50-day Q-U-I-L-T-I-N-G S-N-E-A-K-E-R.S System**. This chapter ensures your quilted sneakers not only look great but also have a polished, professional finish. On **Day 22**, you'll master the art of professional quilted edge finishes, learning how to tidy up seams, edges, and corners for a crisp, clean look. On **Day 23**, you'll focus on sealing and protecting your creations with the right fabric protectants and finishing products, ensuring your sneakers stay durable and weather-resistant. Finally, on **Day 24**, you'll perform quality checks and make final adjustments, ensuring your sneakers meet the highest standards before they're ready to wear or showcase. This chapter equips you with the skills to refine every detail, elevating your quilted sneakers into high-quality, wearable art.

Professional finishing elevates your project from homemade to high-quality handmade.

Day 22: Professional Quilted Edge Finishes

Today is all about clean, professional edge work—one of the most important details for giving your quilted sneakers a polished, high-quality finish. Edges that are smooth, sealed, and secure not only look better but also protect your panels from fraying and help your sneakers last longer.

You've already created something artistic and unique. Now it's time to refine the edges so your final product feels just as strong and well-made as it looks.

Neatly finished edges ensure durability and a refined final look.

A. Step-by-Step Lesson: Finish Edges Like a Pro

1. Assess Each Edge Zone

Look at all exposed fabric edges: around the toe box, side panels, heel, and collar. Decide whether each edge needs to be tucked, stitched, trimmed, or sealed based on its material and placement.

2. Fold Under and Stitch

For raw fabric edges, fold them under ¼ inch and secure with a clean topstitch. This is ideal for cotton panels and provides a durable, no-fray finish.

3. Apply Bias Tape or Binding

Use pre-made or self-cut bias tape to wrap and enclose edges for a clean look. Stitch in place by hand or machine. This method adds a professional, piped edge and works well for curves or corners.

4. Use Edge Sealant or Fabric Glue

For tricky corners or layered mixed media edges, apply fabric glue or fray check along the raw edge to seal and prevent unraveling. Let it dry completely before wearing.

5. Cover with Decorative Stitching

A zigzag or blanket stitch can add both reinforcement and style. Choose matching or contrast thread depending on the look you want.

B. Why This Matters

Finishing the edges properly takes your sneakers from homemade to high-end. It shows you've taken time to care for every detail and ensures your work is built to last. Polished edges also create clean transitions between materials, making the entire design more cohesive and refined.

C. Tips & Creative Ideas

- **Use Matching Bias Tape**: Coordinate with your fabric for seamless finishing.

- **Add Faux Leather or Ribbon Trim**: For a designer touch around the collar or side panel edges.

- **Practice on Scrap Fabric**: Get your folds, stitches, and sealants right before applying to your sneakers.
- **Mix Techniques**: Combine binding and glue sealing where needed for tricky spots.

D. Reflection & Motivation

Today you added polish and professionalism to your handcrafted creation. These final touches are what elevate your sneakers from creative to collectible. Tomorrow, you'll take one last step to protect your work and ensure it stays beautiful through real-world wear. You're nearly finished—and your project is looking incredible.

Day 23: Seal & Protect Your Quilted Sneakers

Now that your quilted sneakers are fully assembled and beautifully finished, it's time to protect all that hard work. Today's focus is sealing and safeguarding your creation—ensuring it's ready to handle everyday wear, weather, and long-term use.

Preserving your sneakers is just as important as designing them. With the right protective methods, your fabrics, stitching, and embellishments will stay vibrant, secure, and wearable for many walks to come.

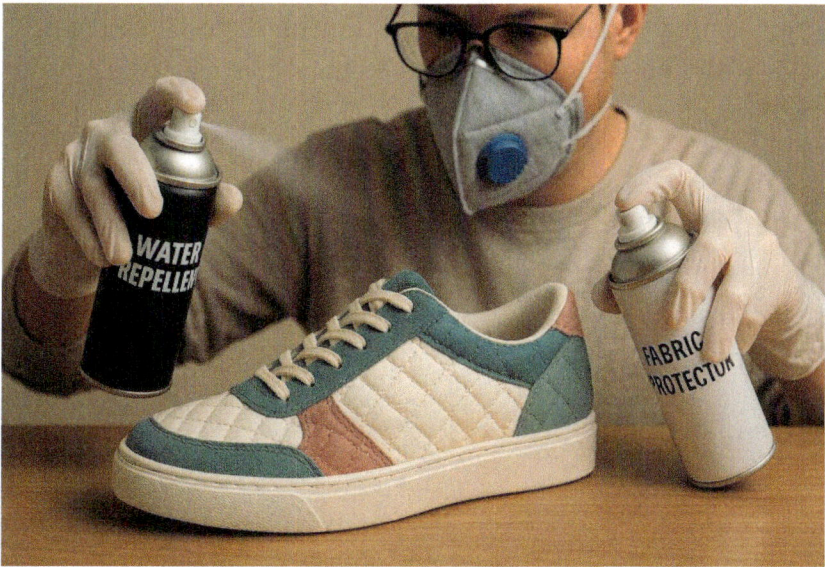

Protect your creation from the elements with the right finishing sprays and sealants.

A. Step-by-Step Lesson: Apply Protection the Right Way

1. Clean the Surface Gently

Use a lint roller or soft brush to remove dust and threads. If needed, lightly dab any smudges with a damp cloth—avoid soaking the fabric. Make sure your sneakers are dry before sealing.

2. Choose a Fabric-Safe Protective Spray

Look for waterproofing or protective sprays designed for fabric or canvas shoes. Read labels carefully to ensure they won't stain or stiffen the materials. Test on a scrap piece of your quilt fabric first.

3. Apply Evenly in a Well-Ventilated Area

Hold the spray about 6–8 inches away and apply in light, even coats. Cover the entire fabric area of the sneaker, including seams and stitched zones. Allow it to dry fully—usually about 24 hours.

4. Seal Additional Elements Separately

If you've used leather, paint, vinyl, or embellishments, consider sealing those parts with specialized products like leather conditioners, clear sealants, or mod podge (for decorative accents only).

5. Repeat As Needed

For long-term durability, reapply protective spray every few months or after heavy wear. Always store your sneakers in a clean, dry space to help them last.

B. Why This Matters

Sealing your sneakers protects your fabric from dirt, moisture, and stains—while also preserving color, structure, and stitching. It turns your creative project into a practical, wearable piece that you can enjoy and show off without worry.

C. Tips & Creative Ideas

- **Use Painter's Tape**: Mask off rubber soles and non-quilted areas before spraying.

- **Stuff with Paper**: Insert paper or shoe trees to maintain shape while drying.

- **Protect Before Gifting or Selling**: Always seal before giving or showcasing your sneakers.

- **Use a Hair Dryer on Low**: Help speed up dry time in cool environments (never on high heat).

D. Reflection & Motivation

Today you safeguarded your masterpiece—proof that you care about your craft and your creation's longevity. Your sneakers are now not only stylish and unique but also ready to take on the world.

Tomorrow, you'll perform final checks and make any last adjustments needed before wearing, gifting, or displaying your finished work. You're in the final stretch—your success is sewn in!

Day 24: Quality Checks & Final Adjustments

You've stitched, styled, and sealed your sneakers—now it's time to make sure they're fully ready to wear, gift, or show off. Today is all about quality checks and small adjustments that elevate your work from "done" to "exceptional."

This step gives you a chance to step back, inspect your work, and fine-tune every detail. From comfort to appearance, durability to finishing touches, you'll make sure your quilted sneakers meet the highest standards—yours.

Final checks help catch issues before wearing, gifting, or selling your sneakers.

A. Step-by-Step Lesson: Inspect and Perfect Your Sneakers

1. Perform a Visual Inspection

Examine each sneaker from all angles. Look for loose threads, uneven stitching, exposed glue, or fabric bubbles. Make a note of anything that stands out or feels unfinished.

2. Check Stitch Strength and Panel Hold

Gently tug on quilted panels and embellishments to test their attachment. Reinforce any areas that feel weak with additional stitching or adhesive.

3. Test Comfort and Fit

Slip the sneakers on and walk around. Make sure there are no rough seams, tight spots, or stiff edges. If needed, file down sharp eyelets, add padding inside, or trim bulky seams for comfort.

4. Clean Up Edges and Surfaces

Trim stray threads, wipe off dust or fingerprints, and gently brush the surface to refresh the fabric. A little cleanup can make a big difference in the final presentation.

5. Evaluate Design Consistency

Double-check that left and right sneakers match in theme, color placement, and style. If asymmetry was intentional, make sure it's balanced and visually appealing.

B. Why This Matters

The final adjustments ensure your sneakers are not only beautiful but also functional, durable, and wearable. This step helps catch small issues before they become bigger problems—and it's your opportunity to take pride in every detail of your finished product.

C. Tips & Creative Ideas

- **Use a Fabric Shaver**: Remove fuzz or pilling for a clean finish.

- **Take Final Photos**: Document your work before wear—great for portfolios or social media.

- **Create a Care Tag**: If gifting or selling, include care instructions for cleaning and maintenance.

- **Celebrate the Craft**: Compare your final sneakers to your Day 1 inspiration board—you'll see how far you've come.

D. Reflection & Motivation

Today you made the final touches that elevate your sneakers to their highest potential. You've gone from idea to design, from fabric to footwear—and now your quilted sneakers are ready to step out into the world. Tomorrow, we'll begin exploring next-level techniques that will take your creativity even further. For now, take a moment to appreciate what you've built—this is what handmade excellence looks like.

Chapter 8 Review: G – Guarantee Professional-Level Finishing

Chapter 8 covered **Days 22–24** of your journey through the 50-Day **Q-U-I-L-T-I-N-G S-N-E-A-K-E-R-S** system, focusing on **G – Guarantee Professional-Level Finishing**. This chapter was all about elevating your work from handmade to high-quality by refining the edges, protecting your designs, and completing thorough final inspections. With attention to detail and care, your sneakers now look as polished as they are personal.

Day 22 – Professional Quilted Edge Finishes

- **Clean up raw edges** – Use bias tape, binding, or precision topstitching for crisp, finished lines.

- **Secure seams and borders** – Reinforce areas prone to fraying or stress, especially around curves and corners.

- **Match your finish to your style** – Choose subtle, bold, or decorative edges to complement your design.

- **Maintain structure** – Finishing techniques also help maintain the shape and fit of your panels.

Day 23 – Seal & Protect Your Quilted Sneakers

- **Apply protective treatments** – Use water-resistant sprays or fabric sealants to preserve your work.

- **Protect high-contact zones** – Focus on the toe, heel, and sides where dirt and wear show most.

- **Test on scrap first** – Always test sprays or finishes on extra fabric to avoid discoloration or damage.

- **Add optional linings or layers** – Improve interior comfort and reduce fabric wear from the inside out.

Day 24 – Quality Checks & Final Adjustments

- **Inspect your sneakers closely** – Look for loose threads, uneven stitching, or lifting panels.

- **Wear test (if possible)** – Walk around briefly to check comfort, stability, and fit.

- **Adjust and polish** – Tighten laces, smooth fabric, or add final touches for presentation.

- **Photograph your finished work** – Capture your completed pair in natural light from multiple angles.

By the end of Chapter 8, your quilted sneakers are professionally finished, protected, and ready to be worn, displayed, or shared with pride. In **Chapter 9: S – Sustain & Maintain Quilted Sneakers (Days 25–27)**, you'll learn how to care for your creations, repair them when needed, and store them properly to ensure they last for years to come.

Chapter 9: S – Sustain & Maintain Quilted Sneakers

In Chapter 9, we focus on **S**, which stands for **Sustain** in the **50-day Q-U-I-L-T-I-N-G S-N-E-A-K-E-R.S System**. This chapter ensures that your quilted sneakers stay looking fresh and last for years to come. On **Day 25**, you'll learn how to clean and maintain your sneakers properly, using the right techniques to preserve fabric and stitching. On **Day 26**, you'll dive into repair tips and tricks for long-term wear, giving you the tools to fix minor wear and tear and keep your sneakers in top shape. Finally, on **Day 27**, you'll explore effective sneaker storage solutions, learning how to store your quilted sneakers in a way that prevents damage and helps them maintain their shape. This chapter provides the essential knowledge for maintaining your craftsmanship and ensuring that your quilted sneakers remain a statement piece for the long haul.

Keeping your quilted sneakers clean ensures long-term wear and continued pride in your work.

Day 25: Clean & Maintain Your Sneakers Properly

Now that your quilted sneakers are complete, it's important to care for them properly. Today's focus is on cleaning and maintenance—keeping your custom kicks looking sharp and feeling great after every wear.

Because quilted sneakers combine fabric, stitching, and embellishments, they require a little more attention than standard footwear. With a few simple habits, you can extend their life and keep them fresh for years to come.

Clean your sneakers gently to preserve fabric texture and stitch integrity.

A. Step-by-Step Lesson: Clean with Care and Consistency

1. **Remove Laces and Insoles**

Before cleaning, take out your shoelaces and insoles (if removable). This allows for better access and more thorough cleaning. Wash laces separately by hand or in a mesh laundry bag.

2. Brush Off Surface Dirt

Use a soft brush or dry cloth to gently remove dust, dirt, and debris from the fabric and soles. Avoid stiff bristles that might pull threads or damage quilting.

3. Spot Clean with Mild Soap

Mix a few drops of gentle detergent or dish soap with warm water. Dip a soft cloth or sponge in the solution and gently dab stained areas. Do not soak the sneaker—too much water can damage fabric and adhesives.

4. Dry Naturally

After spot cleaning, stuff the sneakers with paper towels or clean rags to help them keep their shape. Let them air dry in a shaded area. Avoid direct sunlight or heat sources, which can cause shrinkage, fading, or glue failure.

5. Freshen Inside with Baking Soda (Optional)

Sprinkle a small amount of baking soda inside your sneakers to absorb odors overnight. Shake it out the next morning before wearing.

B. Why This Matters

Proper cleaning and care preserve your hard work and protect your creative investment. Gentle maintenance keeps your sneakers looking new, smelling fresh, and performing well—so you can enjoy them longer with pride and comfort.

C. Tips & Creative Ideas

- **Use a Fabric Protector Spray**: Reapply periodically for water and stain resistance.

- **Create a Cleaning Kit**: Keep soft brushes, cloths, and gentle soap in one box just for your custom sneakers.

- **Keep a Care Card**: If gifting or selling, include cleaning instructions for the recipient.

- **Rotate Shoes**: Give your sneakers a break between wears to let them breathe and last longer.

D. Reflection & Motivation

You've completed your custom quilted sneakers—and now you know how to keep them looking their best. Caring for your work shows respect for your craft, your creativity, and yourself. Tomorrow, you'll learn how to handle repairs and fix common wear-and-tear issues so your sneakers stay strong over time. You're not just an artist—you're a sneaker care pro in the making.

Day 26: Repair Tips & Tricks for Long-Term Wear

Even the most well-crafted quilted sneakers will experience wear over time. Today's focus is on learning simple repair techniques to extend the life of your custom shoes. From loose threads to lifted panels, knowing how to fix common issues will keep your sneakers looking fresh and functional for years to come.

You've put care into creating something beautiful—now you'll learn how to maintain that quality through easy, effective repairs.

**Quick fixes like patching and reinforcing stitching can extend
your sneakers' lifespan.**

A. Step-by-Step Lesson: Repair With Confidence

1. Tighten Loose Threads

If stitching begins to unravel, use a needle and matching thread to
reinforce the original seam. Backstitch over the area for strength.
Trim excess threads cleanly with sharp scissors.

2. Reattach Lifting Panels

If a quilted panel starts peeling away, clean the surface underneath,
then apply a small amount of fabric glue or shoe adhesive. Press
firmly and let dry fully before wearing again.

3. Fix Fabric Frays

Dab fray check or clear fabric glue along raw edges to stop further
unraveling. You can also stitch a small border around the edge using
a whipstitch or zigzag stitch for reinforcement.

4. Patch Worn or Damaged Sections

Cut a small piece of matching or contrasting fabric to create a patch. Use hand stitching or adhesive to secure it in place. Add decorative stitching around the patch for a creative look.

5. Reinforce High-Stress Areas

If parts of the sneaker (like the toe or heel) start to sag or feel weak, layer additional quilting, interfacing, or even an appliqué patch to strengthen the area while adding style.

B. Why This Matters

Knowing how to repair your sneakers keeps them in rotation and prevents small issues from becoming major problems. It also empowers you to experiment with creative solutions—turning repairs into opportunities to refresh or redesign your look.

C. Tips & Creative Ideas

- **Keep a Repair Kit Handy**: Include needles, thread, glue, fabric scraps, and fray check.

- **Use Repairs as Style Features**: Patches and visible stitches can be intentional design elements.

- **Double-Stitch Trouble Spots**: Reinforce seams that experience the most motion or rubbing.

- **Document Repairs**: Track fixes in a journal or sketchbook to learn and improve for future pairs.

D. Reflection & Motivation

Today, you learned how to care for your sneakers with the same intention and creativity you used to design them. These simple fixes keep your work wearable, sustainable, and strong. Tomorrow, we'll explore smart storage solutions that protect your sneakers and preserve their shape and color between wears. You're not just building sneakers—you're building long-term success.

Day 27: Effective Sneaker Storage Solutions

Now that your quilted sneakers are designed, finished, and protected, it's time to think about where and how to store them. Proper storage ensures your sneakers stay clean, hold their shape, and avoid fading, dust, or damage between wears.

Today's goal is to create a space or system that keeps your custom footwear looking fresh, organized, and display-worthy. Whether you wear them regularly or just on special occasions, the right storage setup makes a big difference.

Store sneakers properly to prevent dust buildup, creasing, or moisture damage.

A. Step-by-Step Lesson: Store Your Sneakers with Care

1. Clean Before Storing

Always store your sneakers when they're clean and fully dry. Spot clean them if needed, and brush off any dirt or dust. This prevents staining, odor buildup, and fabric deterioration over time.

2. Use Shoe Trees or Stuffing

Insert shoe trees, rolled towels, or tissue paper inside your sneakers to help them maintain their shape. This is especially important for high-tops or heavily quilted panels that may sag over time.

3. Keep in a Dust-Free Environment

Store your sneakers in a fabric shoe bag, clear plastic box, or on a shelf away from direct sunlight and humidity. Avoid cardboard boxes if moisture is a concern.

4. Avoid Crushing or Stacking

Don't stack other items on top of your quilted sneakers, as it can flatten fabric and stitching. If you store them in a closet, give them their own space to breathe.

5. Label and Rotate

If you create multiple pairs, label each storage container with a photo or name. Rotate your sneakers occasionally if you wear them often to allow fabric time to rest and reduce stress on seams.

B. Why This Matters

Storing your sneakers correctly keeps all your hard work safe—preserving colors, shape, stitching, and structure. It helps prevent avoidable damage and gives your custom creations the long-term care they deserve. A good storage system also makes it easier to share, showcase, or sell your work in the future.

C. Tips & Creative Ideas

- **Display Creatively**: Use a shadow box or open shelving to show off your sneakers as art.

- **DIY Storage Tags**: Attach handmade tags with the sneaker name, design inspiration, or care instructions.

- **Travel Smart**: Use a padded sneaker bag or wrap each shoe in fabric when transporting them.

- **Deodorize Between Wears**: Use cedar shoe inserts or sprinkle baking soda inside between uses.

D. Reflection & Motivation

Today, you created a home for your quilted sneakers—a final step in honoring your craftsmanship. With smart storage, your sneakers are protected, presentable, and always ready for their next moment. Up next: get ready to explore advanced techniques and ideas that will take your creativity even further. You're not just maintaining your work—you're preparing for what's next.

Chapter 9 Review: S – Sustain & Maintain Quilted Sneakers

Chapter 9 covered **Days 25–27** of your journey through the 50-Day **Q-U-I-L-T-I-N-G S-N-E-A-K-E-R-S** system, focusing on **S – Sustain & Maintain Quilted Sneakers**. This chapter taught you how to protect your hard work by keeping your sneakers clean, functional, and long-lasting. From maintenance routines to repair strategies and storage tips, you now have the knowledge to preserve your creations over time.

Day 25 – Clean & Maintain Your Sneakers Properly

- **Use gentle cleaning methods** – Spot clean with a soft brush, mild detergent, and cold water to avoid damaging fabric and stitches.

- **Avoid harsh machine washing** – Preserve structure and detailing by hand-cleaning quilted areas.

- **Protect with routine care** – Wipe down after use and reapply fabric protectant regularly.

- **Maintain laces and liners** – Replace or refresh smaller parts to keep your sneakers looking and feeling new.

Day 26 – Repair Tips & Tricks for Long-Term Wear

- **Fix loose threads or lifting edges** – Use strong adhesives or hand-stitching to reattach worn areas.

- **Patch worn panels creatively** – Cover damage with new fabric pieces, embroidery, or custom appliqués.

- **Reinforce weak spots** – Strengthen stress areas with additional stitches or fabric backing.

- **Keep a mini repair kit** – Include scissors, fabric glue, thread, and swatches to handle repairs on the go.

Day 27 – Effective Sneaker Storage Solutions

- **Store in a cool, dry place** – Avoid direct sunlight, dampness, or extreme heat that can damage fabrics.

- **Use shoe trees or stuffing** – Maintain shape by filling sneakers with paper or form inserts.

- **Keep dust and dirt out** – Use fabric bags or clear boxes to protect while displaying or storing.

- **Label and organize** – If you've made multiple pairs, store with care tags or notes about each design.

By the end of Chapter 9, you've built a care system to ensure your quilted sneakers remain wearable and showcase-worthy. In **Chapter 10: N – Next-Level Quilted Sneaker Techniques (Days 28–30)**, you'll explore advanced creative ideas, combining quilting with other crafts and pushing the boundaries of what's possible with custom sneakers.

Chapter 10: N – Next-Level Quilted Sneaker Techniques

Chapter 10, focusing on **N** for **Next-Level** in the **50-day Q-U-I-L-T-I-N-G S-N-E-A-K-E-R.S System**, takes your quilted sneaker skills to bold new heights. On **Day 28**, you'll experiment with complex quilt patterns, exploring intricate designs that push your creativity and technique to the next level. **Day 29** invites you to combine quilting with other crafts, such as painting or embroidery, to elevate your sneakers with unique, multi-dimensional elements. Finally, on **Day 30**, you'll innovate your quilted sneaker designs, learning how to integrate original elements and signature styles to make your creations stand out. This chapter is all about expanding your skills, thinking outside the box, and setting yourself apart as a true quilted sneaker artist.

Pushing creative boundaries leads to original, standout quilted sneaker designs.

Day 28: Experiment with Complex Quilt Patterns

You've mastered the basics—now it's time to elevate your artistry. Today's focus is on exploring more complex quilt patterns that challenge your skills and expand your creative vision. These intricate designs add layers of meaning, visual texture, and craftsmanship to your sneakers.

Complex patterns require more planning and precision, but they offer powerful payoff. Whether you're aiming for bold visuals or detailed storytelling through your panels, this is where your quilted sneakers start to look like true gallery-worthy pieces.

Complex patterns challenge your precision and open new design possibilities.

A. Step-by-Step Lesson: Level Up Your Quilting Design

1. Explore Advanced Quilt Patterns

Look into patterns like **Mariner's Compass**, **Double Wedding Ring**, **Cathedral Window**, or **Feathered Star**. These involve curves, detailed piecing, and multi-step layouts that can be adapted to small sneaker panels.

2. Choose One Focal Area

Start with one section of the sneaker to feature the complex design— like the side panel or tongue. Keeping it focused avoids visual overload and simplifies execution.

3. Use a Foundation Paper Piecing (FPP) Method

FPP is ideal for precise angles and shapes. Print your design on paper, stitch fabric directly onto the paper following number order, then remove the paper backing before assembly.

4. Scale It Down Thoughtfully

Adjust pattern proportions to fit small sneaker sections. Use fewer blocks or reduce repetition while preserving the overall look and structure.

5. Combine with Simpler Panels

Use solid or simple quilted sections around the complex pattern to balance the design and let your focal area shine.

B. Why This Matters

Complex quilt patterns push your limits and open new doors creatively. They elevate your craftsmanship, show off your growth, and make your sneakers true conversation pieces. This is the difference between "DIY" and "design innovation."

C. Tips & Creative Ideas

- **Color Code Your Pieces**: Use colored pencil plans to stay organized while piecing.
- **Layer Fabrics Strategically**: Use contrast fabrics to highlight the structure of the pattern.

- **Use Metallic or Variegated Thread**: Adds detail and dimension to complex blocks.

- **Document Your Process**: Take photos of each step—you'll want to look back and share your technique.

D. Reflection & Motivation

Today, you reached a new level of quilting artistry. Tackling a complex design shows not only skill, but confidence in your craft. Tomorrow, you'll explore how to combine quilting with other creative hobbies to make even more unique and personal sneakers. You're building something that's truly one of a kind—keep going strong.

Day 29: Combine Quilting with Other Crafts

Quilting is a powerful foundation—but it becomes even more exciting when combined with other creative skills. Today's focus is on blending quilting with other crafts like painting, dyeing, weaving, beading, or digital design to make your sneakers truly one-of-a-kind.

This is your opportunity to cross creative boundaries, experiment freely, and merge multiple passions into a wearable masterpiece. Combining crafts not only boosts your design range but also helps you develop a unique personal style.

Mix mediums like painting, beading, or leatherwork to elevate your sneakers into hybrid art pieces.

A. Step-by-Step Lesson: Blend Crafts Seamlessly

1. Choose a Complementary Craft

Pick one craft that naturally pairs with quilting and works on a sneaker scale:

- o **Fabric painting** for detailed artwork or textures
- o **Tie-dye or dip-dye** for ombré or gradient fabric effects
- o **Beadwork or sequins** for sparkle and dimension
- o **Hand lettering or stamping** for quotes or phrases
- o **Weaving or macramé accents** for fringe, lacing, or collar detail

2. Select the Right Application Area

Decide where your extra craftwork will go—on the quilted panel itself, as an accent around seams, or layered on top. Test materials first to make sure they adhere well and won't fray or stiffen.

3. Coordinate with Quilted Elements

Use your quilting colors, shapes, or textures to guide the new craft. For example, use a painted line that follows your stitched design or a beaded motif that mirrors your quilt pattern.

4. Attach or Apply With Care

Use the correct tools and adhesives based on your medium:

- Fabric paint should dry completely before handling
- Beads should be stitched securely with strong thread
- Embellishments should be flexible enough to move with the sneaker

5. Balance the Design

Don't let one technique overpower the rest. Use restraint to let each medium enhance your quilting—not compete with it. Think of the added craft as a highlight, not the whole show.

B. Why This Matters

Combining crafts allows you to personalize your sneakers beyond quilting alone. It fuses your full range of talents into one expression and turns your shoes into true mixed-media art. It also makes your work stand out in a world of cookie-cutter design.

C. Tips & Creative Ideas

- **Paint First, Quilt After**: If you're painting fabric, do it before cutting and stitching to avoid smudges.

- **Use Handwriting**: Write quotes or initials with a fabric pen for a personal message.

- **Try Fabric Transfers**: Print digital art onto transfer sheets and iron onto panels.

- **Create Matching Accessories**: Use leftover fabric and crafting techniques to make a matching hat, wristband, or patch.

D. Reflection & Motivation

Today you fused quilting with other creative talents—and opened the door to endless new ideas. Combining crafts makes your work multidimensional and unmistakably yours. Tomorrow, we'll wrap up this chapter by exploring how to innovate your sneaker design process for future projects. You've come so far—now it's time to think like a true creator.

Day 30: Innovate Your Quilted Sneaker Designs

Innovation is where artistry meets imagination—and today, you'll focus on how to continually evolve your quilted sneaker designs. Whether you've made one pair or plan to make many more, thinking like an innovator means pushing boundaries, trying new ideas, and finding your creative edge.

This day is about thinking beyond what you've already done and envisioning what's possible. Your goal is to explore new shapes, concepts, and techniques that reflect your voice as a designer and open new doors for future creations.

Let your imagination lead as you develop new signature looks in quilted footwear.

A. Step-by-Step Lesson: Think Like a Sneaker Innovator

1. Analyze What You've Created So Far

Lay out your finished sneaker or review photos of your process. What worked well? What would you change next time? Identify 2–3 standout features and 2 areas where you'd like to improve.

2. Explore Unconventional Design Ideas

Brainstorm wild or unexpected concepts:

- o Reversible quilted panels
- o Glow-in-the-dark stitching
- o Sneaker designs inspired by music, cities, or moods
- o Sustainable upcycled materials
- o Themed collections or storytelling sneakers

3. Sketch or Mood Board Your Next Idea

Create a rough sketch or collage that outlines your next-level concept. Focus on the feeling, the theme, or the technical twist you want to explore. Give it a name or title to solidify the idea.

4. Challenge One Element

Pick one part of the process to reimagine—fabric choice, quilting style, construction method, or color palette. Push yourself to experiment beyond your comfort zone in the next pair you make.

5. Document Your Design Thinking

Start a dedicated notebook or digital file to collect and reflect on your evolving ideas. Add sketches, thoughts, swatches, or quotes that inspire you as you grow your creative practice.

B. Why This Matters

Innovation is what turns a hobby into a lasting creative identity. It keeps your work fresh, exciting, and meaningful—not just for you, but for everyone who sees or wears your sneakers. By thinking beyond the basics, you position yourself as an original voice in the DIY and fashion world.

C. Tips & Creative Ideas

- **Create a Limited Series**: Make a trio of sneakers with one common theme or evolving design.

- **Host a Design Challenge**: Invite friends or fellow crafters to submit fabric or themes to inspire your next pair.

- **Mix Time Periods or Styles**: Blend retro quilt patterns with futuristic materials.

- **Name Each Design**: Treat each sneaker like an art piece—with its own name, story, and vibe.

D. Reflection & Motivation

Today, you stepped into the role of designer and innovator. Your journey has taken you from beginner to builder—and now, to visionary. Next, you'll shift from creating to showcasing, learning how to photograph, share, and celebrate your one-of-a-kind sneakers. Your path is just beginning—and it's already uniquely yours.

Chapter 10 Review: N – Next-Level Quilted Sneaker Techniques

Chapter 10 covered **Days 28–30** of your journey through the 50-Day **Q-U-I-L-T-I-N-G S-N-E-A-K-E-R-S** system, focusing on **N – Next-Level Quilted Sneaker Techniques**. This chapter encouraged you to push creative boundaries, explore intricate designs, and mix media in bold new ways. You stepped beyond the basics and began crafting truly original, experimental pieces that reflect your growth and artistic voice.

Day 28 – Experiment with Complex Quilt Patterns

- **Explore intricate motifs** – Try patterns like cathedral window, hexagon flowers, or paper piecing.

- **Scale patterns to fit sneakers** – Adapt detailed designs to small, curved surfaces with precision.

- **Balance complexity with composition** – Let one standout pattern shine, while keeping supporting elements simple.

- **Challenge your skillset** – Stretch your quilting abilities by working with advanced layouts and symmetry.

Day 29 – Combine Quilting with Other Crafts

- **Blend quilting with other art forms** – Incorporate leatherwork, macramé, painting, or textile collage.

- **Repurpose materials creatively** – Use denim scraps, vintage scarves, or embroidery hoops in unexpected ways.

- **Add handcrafted elements** – Fuse beading, weaving, or stamping into your sneaker panels for a mixed-media effect.

- **Tell a story through technique** – Use your combinations to convey a theme or emotional message.

Day 30 – Innovate Your Quilted Sneaker Designs

- **Break traditional boundaries** – Try asymmetry, deconstruction, or bold fabric layering.

- **Invent your own design signature** – Create a look or detail that sets your sneakers apart from any other maker's.

- **Incorporate cultural or personal symbolism** – Design sneakers that reflect your identity, heritage, or values.

- **Document your creative process** – Capture sketches, photos, and notes to track how your innovation evolves.

By the end of Chapter 10, you've developed the mindset and techniques to explore quilted sneaker design as a true art form. In **Chapter 11: E – Exhibit & Share Your Creations (Days 31–33)**, you'll learn how to showcase your work confidently—whether through photography, online portfolios, or public displays.

Chapter 11: E – Exhibit & Share Your Creations

Chapter 11, focused on **E** for **Exhibit** in the **50-day Q-U-I-L-T-I-N-G S-N-E-A-K-E-R.S System**, empowers you to share your creative journey with the world. On **Day 31**, you'll learn how to photograph your quilted sneakers to capture their detail and artistry, ensuring your work shines through on camera. **Day 32** guides you through creating an online portfolio to showcase your designs, providing a platform for others to see your unique creations and follow your growth. On **Day 33**, you'll explore ways to share your work at events or competitions, connecting with a community of artists and sneaker enthusiasts while expanding your influence. This chapter is designed to help you confidently exhibit your creations, share your passion, and take the next step toward making your quilted sneakers known.

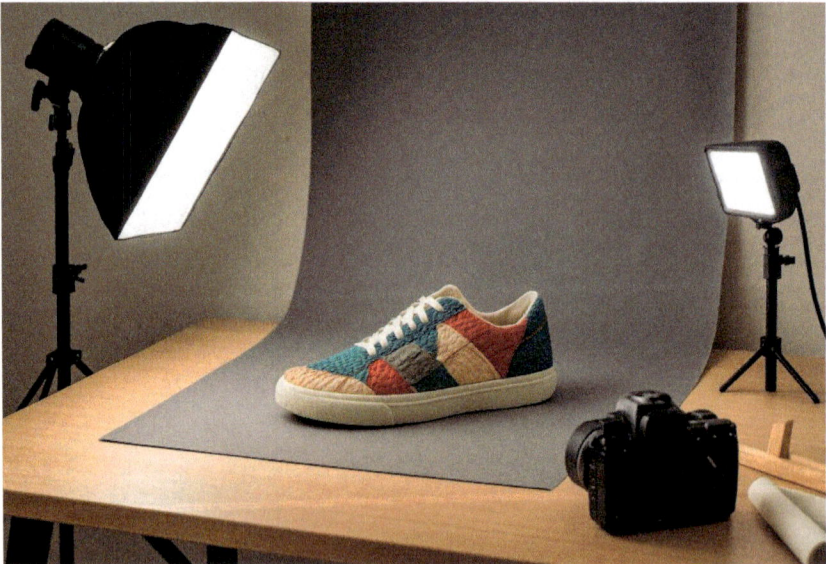

Presenting your work well is just as important as crafting it—document your creations with care.

Day 31: Photograph Your Quilted Sneakers

You've brought your quilted sneakers to life—now it's time to capture them in their best light. Today's focus is learning how to photograph your sneakers in a way that highlights your craftsmanship, details, and design. Whether for personal documentation, social media, or a portfolio, great photos tell the story of your work.

You don't need a professional camera to get professional-looking results. With the right setup, lighting, and framing, you can showcase your sneakers like a pro using just your phone or a simple camera.

Capture your sneaker's best angles to showcase detail and craftsmanship.

A. Step-by-Step Lesson: Take Clean, Creative Photos

1. **Clean and Prep Your Sneakers**

Wipe off dust, fix laces, and make sure your sneakers look fresh. Stuff them with tissue paper or insert shoe trees to hold their shape while shooting.

2. Set Up Good Lighting

Natural daylight is ideal. Shoot near a window or outdoors in shaded sunlight for even lighting. Avoid harsh shadows or artificial yellow light.

3. Choose a Neutral Background

Use a clean, solid background like white poster board, wood floor, fabric drape, or a minimal setting. Let your sneakers stand out— avoid cluttered or distracting spaces.

4. Capture Multiple Angles

Take shots from the side, top, back, and front. Get close-ups of quilting, embroidery, or embellishments. Show detail and texture, especially if you used complex or mixed media elements.

5. Use a Consistent Style

Edit lightly for brightness and clarity if needed, but keep colors accurate. Use the same style and setup for all pairs you photograph to build a cohesive look across your gallery or social posts.

B. Why This Matters

Photographs are how the world sees your work. Clean, well-composed images make your quilted sneakers look professional and showcase your skills. Whether you're selling, gifting, or simply documenting your journey, great photos help others connect with your creativity.

C. Tips & Creative Ideas

- **Use Props or Styling**: Add spools of thread, scissors, or swatches to tell your design story.

- **Shoot "Before and After"**: Show your original sketch next to the finished sneakers.

- **Try On-Foot Shots**: Model your sneakers or have a friend wear them to show fit and style.

- **Use Editing Apps**: Apps like Snapseed, Lightroom Mobile, or VSCO help refine your photos quickly.

D. Reflection & Motivation

Today, you celebrated your work through a new lens—literally. Photography allows you to share your creation with the world and look back on how far you've come. Tomorrow, you'll take those images and build a digital space to showcase your growing body of quilted sneaker art. You're not just creating—you're curating your creative legacy.

Day 32: Create an Online Quilted Sneaker Portfolio

Today you'll take your quilted sneaker photography and build a digital portfolio—a dedicated space to showcase your work, tell your story, and connect with others. Whether you're sharing with friends, starting a creative brand, or exploring business possibilities, an online portfolio gives your work a professional, permanent home.

You don't need to be a tech expert to do this. From simple photo galleries to full websites, there are many easy options to choose from. The goal is to make your work accessible, organized, and uniquely yours.

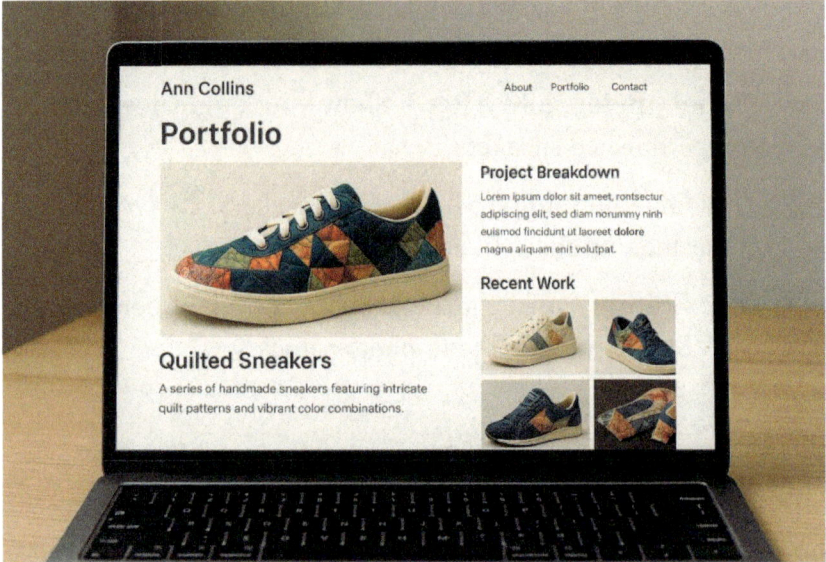

A portfolio builds credibility and allows others to follow and support your creative journey.

A. Step-by-Step Lesson: Build Your Digital Showcase

1. Choose Your Platform

Pick a platform that matches your needs and comfort level:

- o **Instagram or Pinterest** for social, visual-first sharing
- o **Behance or Adobe Portfolio** for design-style galleries
- o **Wix, Squarespace, or WordPress** to create your own website
- o **Etsy or Shopify** if you're planning to sell

2. Organize Your Content

Group your sneakers by theme, collection, or creative style. Add project titles, dates, or sneaker names. Include your best photos from Day 31—use 3–6 shots per project.

3. Write Captions or Descriptions

Briefly share the story behind each pair:

- o Your design inspiration

- o Quilting techniques used

- o Favorite materials or details

- o Any special meaning behind the design

4. Add an "About You" Section

Introduce yourself as a maker. Keep it personal and creative: mention why you started quilting sneakers, what inspires your designs, and what your goals are. Include a photo if you're comfortable.

5. Publish and Share

Once your page or profile is ready, share it with friends, family, or creative communities. Use hashtags and tags to reach others who love quilting, sneakers, or DIY fashion.

B. Why This Matters

An online portfolio gives your creativity a permanent, professional presence. It helps you track your progress, connect with supporters, and open up future opportunities—whether that's collaborations, commissions, or simply sharing your passion with the world.

C. Tips & Creative Ideas

- • **Use a Creative Name**: Give your portfolio or gallery a fun name that reflects your brand or personality.

- **Link Across Platforms**: Add your website link to your social bios, or vice versa.

- **Post Process Shots**: People love seeing behind-the-scenes photos and before/after results.

- **Update Regularly**: Keep your space fresh with new photos, designs, or thoughts as you continue to create.

D. Reflection & Motivation

Today, you took a huge step in becoming not just a maker—but a sharer, a storyteller, and a creative presence in the world. Tomorrow, you'll explore how to go even further by showcasing your work in person at events, contests, or exhibitions. Your journey is growing—and now others can watch it unfold.

Day 33: Showcase Your Work at Events or Competitions

You've created your own custom quilted sneakers, captured them through photography, and built a digital portfolio—now it's time to go public. Today's focus is learning how to share your work at events, exhibitions, and competitions. Whether it's a local art fair, a craft contest, or a sneaker design showcase, presenting your work in person is one of the most rewarding parts of the journey.

Showcasing builds confidence, inspires others, and opens new doors for feedback, networking, and recognition. Even if you're just starting out, there's a place for your creativity to shine.

Sharing your work in public settings connects you with new fans, customers, and collaborators.

A. Step-by-Step Lesson: Prepare to Exhibit Your Sneakers

1. Find the Right Event or Platform

Look for creative opportunities that match your niche:

- Local art walks or craft fairs
- Community quilt or fashion shows
- Sneaker expos or streetwear festivals
- Online design contests or Instagram challenges
- Maker meetups or pop-up markets

2. Prepare a Display Setup

Create a presentation that highlights your sneakers and tells your story. Use shoe stands, photo boards, swatches, or sketches. Include signage with your name, contact info, and QR codes linking to your portfolio.

3. Practice Talking About Your Work

Be ready to share your process, materials, and inspiration. Keep it simple and authentic. People love hearing what makes your work unique—especially when it's handmade and creative.

4. Enter Competitions with Confidence

Submit your best photos or bring your best pair to enter a contest. Read all guidelines carefully and don't be afraid to apply, even if you're new. Every entry is a step forward.

5. Gather Feedback and Connect

Use these events to connect with other creatives and sneaker lovers. Ask questions, accept feedback with curiosity, and offer support to fellow makers.

B. Why This Matters

Sharing your work publicly is a celebration of your creativity. It builds visibility, opens you to new opportunities, and shows others what's possible with quilting and self-expression. Exhibiting also validates your hard work—it's a powerful moment of pride and progress.

C. Tips & Creative Ideas

- **Create a Mini Lookbook**: Print a small photo zine with your designs to hand out.

- **Wear Your Work**: Show off your sneakers by walking the event in them—it's the best conversation starter.

- **Offer Custom Orders**: If you're ready, take inquiries for personalized sneaker designs.

- **Document the Event**: Take photos and videos for your portfolio and social media.

D. Reflection & Motivation

Today, you stepped into the spotlight—not just as a crafter, but as a designer, storyteller, and maker ready to share their vision with the world. From Day 1 to Day 33, you've built something incredible—now you're inspiring others to do the same. Next, you'll take things further by expanding your skills, trying new projects, and evolving your creative voice. Your journey is just getting started.

Chapter 11 Review: E – Exhibit & Share Your Creations

Chapter 11 covered **Days 31–33** of your journey through the 50-Day **Q-U-I-L-T-I-N-G S-N-E-A-K-E-R-S** system, focusing on **E – Exhibit & Share Your Creations**. This chapter helped you take your finished work from private creation to public presentation. Whether online, in-person, or on social media, you learned how to confidently display your quilted sneakers as wearable art—and connect with an audience that appreciates your creativity.

Day 31 – Photograph Your Quilted Sneakers

- **Use natural lighting and clean backgrounds** – Showcase your sneakers with clarity and detail.

- **Capture all angles** – Photograph the toe, heel, sides, and top to highlight panel work and stitching.

- **Show scale and styling** – Use props or model shots to convey how the sneakers fit into everyday style.

- **Edit thoughtfully** – Lightly adjust for brightness, contrast, and color accuracy while staying true to your design.

Day 32 – Create an Online Quilted Sneaker Portfolio

- **Choose your platform** – Build a portfolio using Instagram, a personal website, or platforms like Behance or Etsy.

- **Include project details** – List materials used, inspiration, techniques, and design names.

- **Organize your work** – Display collections or designs by theme, year, or technique to make your growth clear.

- **Tell your story** – Include a short bio and artist statement to help people connect with your creative journey.

Day 33 – Showcase Your Work at Events or Competitions

- **Find local or online opportunities** – Look for art fairs, sneaker conventions, craft shows, or design contests.

- **Prepare a display** – Use clean stands, signage, and branding to make your presentation professional.

- **Engage with your audience** – Share your process and inspiration when speaking with others.

- **Collect feedback and connections** – Use events to build relationships, gain visibility, and grow your reputation.

By the end of Chapter 11, your quilted sneakers are no longer just personal projects—they're portfolio-ready pieces you can proudly share with the world. In **Chapter 12: A – Advance Your Sneaker Quilting Skills (Days 34–36),** you'll stretch even further with advanced projects, matching accessories, and the start of your own creative series.

Chapter 12: A – Advance Your Sneaker Quilting Skills

In Chapter 12, we focus on **A** for **Advance**, an essential step in the **50-day Q-U-I-L-T-I-N-G S-N-E-A-K-E.R.S. System** that takes your creativity to the next level. **Day 34** introduces you to the world of quilting matching accessories, like wallets and bags, so you can expand your designs beyond sneakers and create a cohesive style. On **Day 35**, you'll dive into advanced quilted sneaker projects, challenging your skills and pushing your creativity as you explore intricate techniques. Finally, **Day 36** is about launching your own quilted sneaker series or collection, giving you the tools and inspiration to establish your unique brand and express your artistic vision in a larger way. This chapter is designed to elevate your skills and give you the confidence to create even more stunning, wearable art.

Accessorizing your sneakers helps unify your style and expand your creative output.

Day 34: Quilt Matching Accessories (Wallets, Bags)

Today's step takes your creativity beyond sneakers by creating matching quilted accessories like wallets, pouches, or bags. Coordinated accessories bring cohesion to your work, showcase your branding or personal style, and give you new ways to use leftover fabric and practice your quilting skills on a smaller scale.

Whether you're creating for yourself, a gift, or future customers, these mini projects elevate your presentation and expand your skills in a fun, functional way.

Create complementary accessories to complete your look or offer as matching sets.

A. Step-by-Step Lesson: Make Matching Accessories

1. Choose a Simple, Useful Project

Start with beginner-friendly accessories that match your sneaker theme:

- Small zipper pouch
- Mini wallet or card holder
- Crossbody bag
- Drawstring sneaker dust bag
- Keychain or fabric wristlet

2. Use Your Sneaker Fabric Scraps

Pull leftover quilted pieces or coordinating fabrics from your main sneaker project. This adds continuity and helps reduce waste while reinforcing your visual theme.

3. Follow a Basic Quilted Pattern

Create a small quilt sandwich (fabric + batting + backing), quilt with your favorite pattern, and cut out your accessory shape. Use simple straight stitching or decorative stitches to match your sneaker detailing.

4. Assemble Carefully with Clean Finishing

Use zippers, snaps, or fold-over elastic to secure your pieces. Line your accessory with smooth fabric and finish edges with bias tape, binding, or topstitching to keep it looking professional.

5. Add Personal Touches

Embroider your initials, stitch a patch, or add an embellishment that ties into your sneaker's story. These little touches enhance the uniqueness of your set.

B. Why This Matters

Creating matching accessories strengthens your design skills and brand identity. It gives your quilted sneakers a lifestyle feel—where every item reflects a cohesive, creative point of view. Plus, accessories are quick wins that boost your confidence and stretch your imagination.

C. Tips & Creative Ideas

- **Use a Color Theme**: Match thread and fabric choices for a unified look.

- **Create a "Sneaker Care Kit" Pouch**: Use it to store wipes, laces, or polish.

- **Make It Gift-Ready**: Pair a sneaker set with a quilted pouch and a custom care card.

- **Experiment with Closures**: Try zippers, Velcro, buttons, or magnetic snaps for variety.

D. Reflection & Motivation

Today, you expanded your vision and gave your creativity a new outlet. Making matching accessories is more than a fun extra—it's a smart way to use your materials, practice techniques, and explore your style. Tomorrow, you'll take things even further by tackling more advanced sneaker quilting projects. You're growing fast—and your creativity is just getting started.

Day 35: Try Advanced Quilted Sneaker Projects

Today's challenge is to push your skills further by tackling advanced quilted sneaker projects. These next-level builds may involve more complex designs, unconventional materials, or unique construction techniques that test your creativity and craftsmanship. Whether you're experimenting with high-top builds, intricate panels, or hybrid styles, this is your chance to take things to the next tier.

Advanced projects require patience and problem-solving—but they also lead to stunning results that feel original, polished, and truly one of a kind.

Take on larger, more complex projects to refine your skills and stretch your abilities.

A. Step-by-Step Lesson: Level Up Your Sneaker Builds

1. Choose an Advanced Project Concept

Select a more ambitious design to work on, such as:

- **High-top sneakers** with extended quilt panels

- **Layered or multi-fabric panels** that involve more seams and stitch planning

- **Convertible sneakers** with removable or interchangeable quilt pieces

- **Fully themed sneakers** (e.g., seasons, stories, music, pop culture)

2. Create a More Detailed Design Plan

Sketch a more complex layout or use digital tools to map your idea. Break the sneaker into smaller quilting zones for more control. Add notes on layering, stitch types, and how to transition between sections.

3. Test Construction on Scrap Fabric

Before committing to your final sneaker, test parts of your new design on scrap fabric or a sample base. This helps you fine-tune your technique and avoid major issues later.

4. Use Advanced Quilting Techniques

Incorporate trapunto, foundation paper piecing, detailed embroidery, or texture layering to make your panels stand out. Don't rush—plan your quilting line by line for the cleanest results.

5. Assemble with Precision and Care

As advanced designs often involve more bulk and shaping, take extra care when trimming, attaching, and sealing your panels. Reinforce stress points and check for both structure and comfort as you build.

B. Why This Matters

Challenging yourself with advanced builds helps you grow exponentially as a maker. You'll learn how to adapt, problem-solve, and refine your techniques while developing your signature style. These projects also position you as a serious creative force— someone who's not afraid to think big and try new things.

C. Tips & Creative Ideas

- **Create a Mock Pair**: Use inexpensive or old sneakers to test your advanced ideas first.

- **Use Layered Templates**: Build complex designs in parts, then combine for a cleaner assembly.

- **Mix Media Thoughtfully**: Try leather, mesh, or unexpected textures with your quilt blocks.

- **Document Every Step**: Advanced builds are great for content—capture your process in photos or video.

D. Reflection & Motivation

Today, you proved you're ready for more—more detail, more risk, and more creativity. Tackling advanced projects sets you apart and shows how far you've come since Day 1. Tomorrow, you'll take everything you've learned and channel it into a larger vision: launching your own sneaker series or creative collection. You're not just making sneakers anymore—you're building your legacy.

Day 36: Launch a Quilted Sneaker Series or Collection

You've created, refined, and pushed your skills to new heights—now it's time to think bigger. Today's focus is launching a **quilted sneaker series or collection**, a themed set of custom sneakers that showcase your vision, style, and storytelling. Whether for fun, display, or future business, a collection helps you grow as a designer and leave a lasting creative mark.

A cohesive series transforms your one-off creations into a meaningful body of work that reflects your journey, passion, and evolution.

Build a full collection to express your creativity through cohesive storytelling in footwear.

A. Step-by-Step Lesson: Build and Launch Your Sneaker Collection

1. Define a Theme or Concept

Choose a concept that excites you. It could be based on:

- **Seasons** (spring, summer, fall, winter)

- **Emotions or moods** (joy, boldness, calm, rebellion)

- **Music, art, or culture** (albums, artists, countries, fashion eras)

- **Stories or symbols** (travel, transformation, self-growth)

2. Plan a 3–5 Pair Series

Sketch or outline 3–5 unique sneaker designs that relate to your theme. Each pair should stand alone but also feel connected as part of the overall narrative or visual language.

3. Create a Design & Color Palette

Choose 2–3 main colors or patterns to weave throughout the collection. Keep fabric types and quilting styles consistent where possible to unify the look.

4. Document and Present the Collection

As you build the series, photograph each step and completed pair. Create a title for the collection and write a short description for each sneaker—include the meaning, techniques used, and how it fits into the bigger theme.

5. Share or Showcase Your Series

Post your full collection online, submit it to an art show or craft expo, or create a mini digital lookbook. You could even design a logo or brand name for your series if you plan to grow your audience.

B. Why This Matters

Launching a series takes your work from individual projects to a true creative portfolio. It reflects your growth, depth, and dedication—helping you build a signature voice as a quilted sneaker designer. It also opens the door to exciting opportunities like collaborations, commissions, or product lines.

C. Tips & Creative Ideas

- **Name Each Pair**: Give each sneaker in the series a title to reinforce the story.

- **Build a Display Kit**: Create stands, info cards, or a backdrop for showcasing your collection.

- **Create Limited Editions**: Reproduce your favorite pair with slight variations for future projects.

- **Add Matching Accessories**: Include pouches or bags to enhance the collection's depth.

D. Reflection & Motivation

Today, you stepped into your role as a creative visionary. A collection is more than sneakers—it's your artistic voice, stitched together one panel at a time. You've built skills, expressed your ideas, and shared your heart through your hands. Tomorrow, we'll explore ways to connect with communities and share your expertise with others. You're no longer just making—you're building a legacy.

Chapter 12 Review: A – Advance Your Sneaker Quilting Skills

Chapter 12 covered **Days 34–36** of your journey through the 50-Day **Q-U-I-L-T-I-N-G S-N-E-A-K-E-R-S** system, focusing on **A – Advance Your Sneaker Quilting Skills**. This chapter challenged you to push your creative boundaries by expanding your sneaker quilting projects, experimenting with new techniques, and planning for future collections. You've now reached a point where your skills are ready for more complex, professional-level work that can elevate your craft to new heights.

Day 34 – Quilt Matching Accessories (Wallets, Bags)

- **Expand beyond sneakers** – Design matching accessories like wallets, bags, or keychains that complement your quilted sneakers.

- **Use leftover fabric creatively** – Repurpose scraps from your sneaker designs to make coordinated accessories.

- **Practice on smaller projects** – Learn how to scale your techniques for smaller surfaces and intricate stitching.

- **Create signature items** – Build a collection of quilted accessories that reflect the same design ethos as your sneakers.

Day 35 – Try Advanced Quilted Sneaker Projects

- **Tackle larger or more detailed designs** – Experiment with multi-layered or mixed-media sneaker styles.

- **Use more advanced techniques** – Incorporate free-motion quilting, trapunto, or advanced embroidery for extra dimension.

- **Design for function and art** – Push the limits of both comfort and visual appeal, experimenting with unusual shapes or fabrics.

- **Build a more complex portfolio** – Each advanced project should push you further as an artist, expanding both your skill set and creative vision.

Day 36 – Launch a Quilted Sneaker Series or Collection

- **Plan your collection** – Develop a theme for your series, whether it's based on seasons, emotions, or artistic concepts.

- **Create cohesion across designs** – Ensure that each pair within the collection shares key design elements or common colors.

- **Photograph and present professionally** – Document your collection with high-quality images and well-crafted descriptions to showcase its uniqueness.

- **Prepare for sale or display** – Share your collection with the public, either through online platforms or local events, to begin building your brand and reputation.

By the end of Chapter 12, you're not just mastering quilting techniques—you're applying them to create complete collections and advanced projects. In **Chapter 13: K – Knowledge Sharing & Community (Days 37–39)**, you'll start connecting with the broader quilting and sneaker communities, teaching others, and sharing your journey to inspire the next generation of creators.

Chapter 13: K – Knowledge Sharing & Community

Chapter 13, centered on **K** for **Knowledge Sharing**, is an essential part of the **50-day Q-U-I-L-T-I-N-G S-N-E-A-K-E-R.S. System**, designed to inspire you to connect, collaborate, and spread your creativity. **Day 37** focuses on joining quilted sneaker communities, both online and in person, to learn from others, exchange ideas, and expand your creative circle. On **Day 38**, you'll learn how to teach others to quilt sneakers, sharing your newfound expertise and helping others discover this craft. Finally, **Day 39** encourages you to share your personal journey and creations online, using social media or personal blogs to inspire a wider audience and build a community around your work. This chapter emphasizes the importance of giving back, learning from others, and creating a supportive network as you continue your artistic journey.

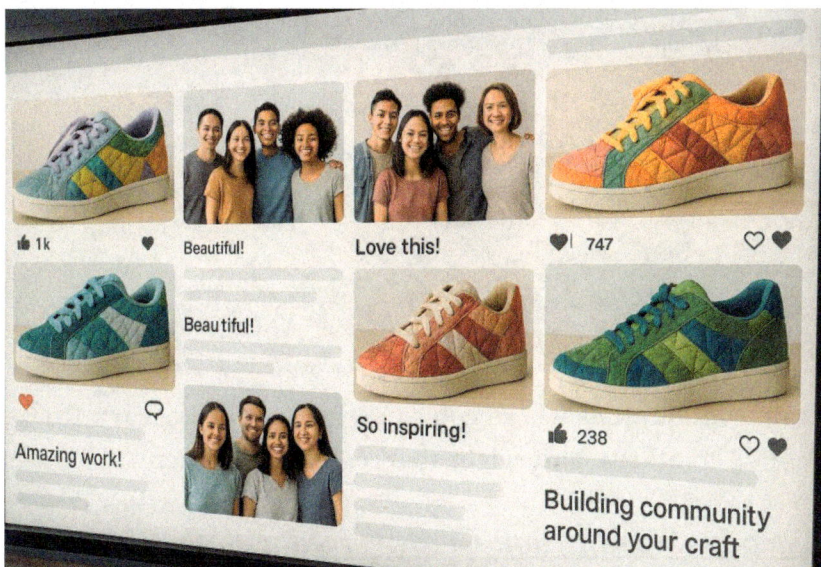

Building community around your craft helps you stay inspired and keep growing.

Day 37: Connect with Quilted Sneaker Communities

Quilting sneakers may start as a solo creative project, but it becomes even more rewarding when you connect with others who share your passion. Today's focus is finding and engaging with communities—online and offline—where you can learn, share, collaborate, and grow together.

Building community not only inspires your creativity but also helps you find support, visibility, and opportunities you might not have discovered on your own.

Join communities where you can share progress, learn from others, and celebrate creativity together.

A. Step-by-Step Lesson: Get Involved with the Creative Community

1. **Find Your People Online**

Search for sneaker design groups, quilting communities, or creative DIY circles on platforms like:

- o **Instagram**: Follow and interact with creators using hashtags like #quiltedsneakers, #customsneakers, or #textileart
- o **Reddit**: Join threads in r/Sneakers, r/quilting, or r/diy
- o **Facebook Groups**: Look for craft, sewing, or sneaker customization groups
- o **Discord Servers**: Many makers host live discussions and collabs in private servers

2. **Attend Local Creative Events**

Look for local maker fairs, art meetups, quilting guilds, or sneaker expos in your area. Attend to observe, participate, or even show off your work in person.

3. **Join Online Courses or Workshops**

Look for virtual classes in quilting, embroidery, shoe customization, or small-batch fashion design. These often include forums or group chats for ongoing connection.

4. **Give and Receive Feedback**

Share your work-in-progress or final designs and ask for feedback. Support others by commenting, liking, and encouraging their creations. Collaboration starts with kindness and curiosity.

5. **Stay Active and Curious**

Community isn't just about following—it's about contributing. Ask questions, share tips, post your process, and celebrate wins (big and small) alongside others.

B. Why This Matters

Connecting with others turns your personal project into part of a larger creative movement. It motivates you to keep growing, opens the door to collaborations, and reminds you that your work matters—because it inspires someone else, too.

C. Tips & Creative Ideas

- **Start Your Own Hashtag**: Create a unique tag for your sneaker series or brand and invite others to use it.

- **Comment with Intention**: Share real thoughts—not just emojis—to make meaningful connections.

- **Host a Mini Challenge**: Invite fellow creators to remix one of your designs or themes.

- **Create a Maker's Journal**: Document your favorite conversations, ideas, or lessons learned from the community.

D. Reflection & Motivation

Today you took your passion and turned it into connection. The creative world is filled with people just like you—curious, expressive, and eager to grow. By joining a community, you gain more than feedback or followers—you gain a network of inspiration and support. Tomorrow, we'll take that even further by helping you become the teacher and guide for others. You're not just a maker—you're becoming a mentor.

Day 38: Teach Others to Quilt Sneakers

Today is all about giving back and lifting others by teaching the skills you've developed. Sharing your knowledge—whether casually with a friend or formally through workshops or content—solidifies your expertise and spreads the joy of quilted sneaker design. Teaching not only helps others grow but also strengthens your own understanding, creativity, and confidence.

Everyone starts somewhere, and your journey can inspire someone else to start theirs.

Teaching your craft helps others grow while deepening your own skills and confidence.

A. Step-by-Step Lesson: Become a Quilt-Sneaker Guide

1. Decide How You Want to Teach

Choose a teaching method that feels comfortable and fun:

- **In-person demo** for a friend, school, or local event
- **Live workshop** (online or local craft store/community center)
- **Step-by-step video** for YouTube, Instagram Reels, or TikTok

- o **Photo tutorial or blog post** outlining a specific technique

2. Pick a Beginner-Friendly Topic

Start with something simple and achievable, such as:

- o How to create a basic quilted panel
- o Choosing fabric and prepping a sneaker base
- o Decorative stitching for sneaker panels
- o Attaching fabric to sneakers cleanly

3. Break Down the Process Clearly

Write out or outline each step in simple terms. Include materials needed, time required, and beginner tips. Use visuals or examples wherever possible to help your learners follow along.

4. Engage and Encourage Learners

Be supportive, answer questions, and celebrate progress. Share your beginner mistakes and lessons learned—it makes you relatable and approachable.

5. Create Shareable Materials

Offer a printable guide, a digital pattern, or even a small freebie (like a swatch chart or checklist). Giving tools helps people feel ready to try and succeed on their own.

B. Why This Matters

Teaching others spreads creativity and builds a culture of sharing, innovation, and connection. It shows that your work has impact beyond the product itself—and helps you find new fulfillment as a mentor, artist, and leader in this space.

C. Tips & Creative Ideas

- **Host a "Sneaker Quilting 101" Day** with friends or in your community

- **Create a Mini Ebook or PDF Guide** with photos from your process

- **Offer Sneaker Quilting Kits** with fabric scraps, patterns, and starter tools

- **Feature Student Work** on your portfolio or social channels to celebrate others

D. Reflection & Motivation

Today, you became more than a maker—you became a guide. Teaching empowers others to create, and it transforms your journey into a legacy. You never know whose creativity you'll unlock by simply showing what's possible. Tomorrow, you'll wrap up this chapter by sharing your full journey online. Your voice is strong—now it's time to share it with the world.

Day 39: Share Your Quilted Sneaker Journey Online

You've come a long way—from learning the basics to creating, innovating, and even teaching others. Today's focus is reflecting on that journey and **sharing it online** to inspire, connect, and celebrate your progress. Your story matters—not just the finished products, but the learning process, the wins, the struggles, and the growth along the way.

Whether you post a single photo, write a blog, or create a video series, putting your journey out into the world adds meaning to your craft and motivates others to start their own.

Share Your Quilted Sneaker Journey Online

DAY 1
Sketching out design ideas

DAY 5
Cutting fabric pieces

DAY 14
Quilting the upper

DAY 39
Finished quilted sneakers!

Share your journey to inspire others and document your growth as a sneaker artist.

Share your journey to inspire others and document your growth as a sneaker artist.

A. Step-by-Step Lesson: Tell Your Story Authentically

1. Choose Your Platform

Pick a platform that fits your voice and audience:

- **Instagram** for photos and short captions
- **TikTok or YouTube** for video storytelling
- **Blog or Medium** for deeper written reflections
- **Pinterest** or **Facebook Groups** to reach hobbyist and DIY audiences

2. Share the Full Journey

Include more than just finished products. Share:

- o Your "why" for starting
- o A photo of your first sketch or Day 1 sneakers
- o In-progress shots, failed experiments, and breakthroughs
- o Reflections on how you've grown creatively and technically

3. Add a Personal Touch

Use your own voice. Whether it's playful, professional, or emotional—let it be real. Talk about challenges you overcame and moments that made you proud.

4. Invite Others to Engage

Ask questions like:

- o "What do you think of this design?"
- o "Which pair is your favorite?"
- o "Ever thought about quilting your own sneakers?" This turns your post into a conversation, not just a broadcast.

5. Use Hashtags and Tags Thoughtfully

Help others discover your journey with relevant hashtags like #QuiltedSneakers, #SneakerCustoms, #MakerJourney, #DIYFashion, or niche tags based on your style.

B. Why This Matters

Sharing your journey makes your creativity visible. It builds community, boosts confidence, and reminds others—and yourself— that progress matters more than perfection. Your story could be the spark that inspires someone else to start creating.

C. Tips & Creative Ideas

- **Do a Before & After Post**: Show Day 1 vs. Day 39 for an amazing visual transformation

- **Create a Carousel or Reel**: Use music and captions to walk people through your journey

- **Write a Reflective Caption**: Keep it honest, proud, and hopeful for the future

- **Pin Your Story**: Make your journey post the first thing people see on your profile

D. Reflection & Motivation

Today, you took a step that many creators overlook: honoring and sharing your journey. Every stitch, photo, and lesson has brought you here—and by opening up your story, you invite others to grow with you. Tomorrow, you'll begin your final chapter—celebrating everything you've achieved and planning what's next. Your voice is out there now, and it's just the beginning.

Chapter 13 Review: K – Knowledge Sharing & Community

Chapter 13 covered **Days 37–39** of your journey through the 50-Day **Q-U-I-L-T-I-N-G S-N-E-A-K-E-R-S** system, focusing on **K – Knowledge Sharing & Community**. This chapter encouraged you to go beyond personal creation and share your skills, experiences, and creativity with the larger quilting and sneaker communities. You learned how to connect, teach, and document your journey in ways that inspire others while strengthening your own practice.

Day 37 – Connect with Quilted Sneaker Communities

- **Find your people** – Look for online and local communities on Instagram, Reddit, Facebook, or Discord where quilted sneaker makers gather.

- **Engage with others** – Like, comment, and share tips with other makers. Be an active participant in the community.

- **Ask for feedback** – Connect with experienced creators for advice, critiques, and inspiration to keep growing.

- **Collaborate and support** – Work on joint projects or collaborate with others to expand your creativity and reach.

Day 38 – Teach Others to Quilt Sneakers

- **Share what you've learned** – Host tutorials or share your techniques through blog posts, videos, or live streams.

- **Start small** – Begin by teaching a beginner-level technique, focusing on clear, step-by-step instructions.

- **Encourage beginners** – Help others feel confident in their ability to start quilting sneakers, offering encouragement and support.

- **Build your teaching style** – Develop your own approach to teaching that fits your personality and strengths.

Day 39 – Share Your Quilted Sneaker Journey Online

- **Document your creative process** – Share photos, stories, and reflections about your journey on platforms like Instagram, TikTok, or YouTube.

- **Be transparent** – Show your successes and failures to make your journey relatable and inspiring to others.

- **Engage with your followers** – Answer questions, ask for feedback, and create a supportive online space for sneaker quilters.

- **Celebrate your milestones** – Share key moments such as completing a project, reaching a new skill level, or launching a collection.

By the end of Chapter 13, you've begun building your presence within the quilting and sneaker communities. You've shared your creativity, taught others, and documented your process in a way that can inspire, connect, and teach. In **Chapter 14: E – Embrace Your Quilting Journey (Days 40–43)**, you'll reflect on your growth, set future goals, and continue to find joy in the journey ahead.

Chapter 14: E – Embrace Your Quilting Journey

In Chapter 14, the focus is on **E** for **Embrace Your Quilting Journey**, a vital part of the **50-day Q-U-I-L-T-I-N-G S-N-E-A-K-E-R.S. System**. This chapter guides you to reflect on your creative progress and growth. **Day 40** encourages you to pause and look back at how far you've come, recognizing both the skills you've mastered and the personal milestones you've reached. On **Day 41**, you'll celebrate your accomplishments and the unique quilted sneakers you've created, marking your journey with pride. **Day 42** helps you set new, exciting goals for the future, ensuring your creative path remains vibrant and fulfilling. Finally, **Day 43** emphasizes the importance of consistency, urging you to continue nurturing your creative practice and stay connected to your craft. This chapter serves as both a reflective pause and a springboard for future creative endeavors.

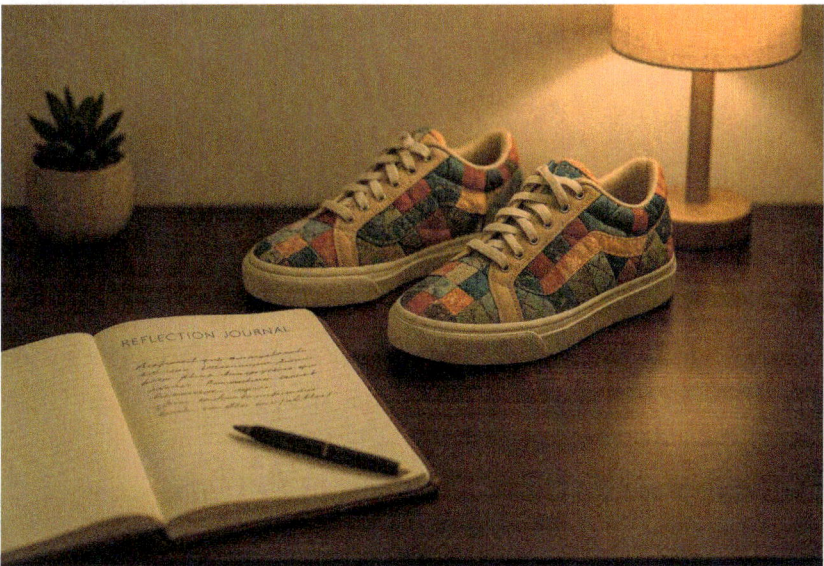

Take time to reflect, recharge, and renew your creative spark after completing a major project.

Day 40: Reflect on Your Progress and Growth

You've reached Day 40 of your 50-day journey—and today is all about looking back. Reflection is a powerful tool that allows you to see how far you've come, what you've learned, and how much you've grown as a maker, artist, and creative thinker.

You've built more than quilted sneakers. You've built confidence, courage, and your own creative voice. Let's take a moment to acknowledge and honor that growth.

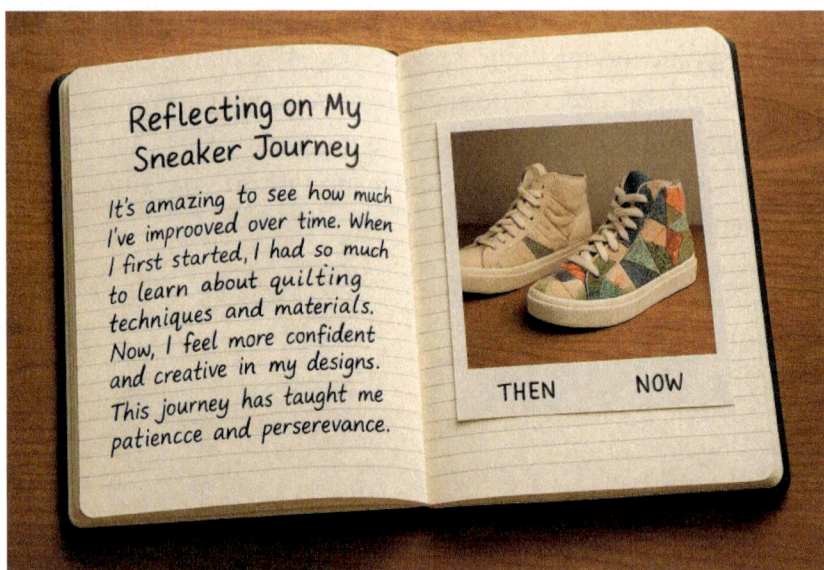

Looking back at your progress reveals how far you've come and what you've learned.

A. Step-by-Step Lesson: Reflect with Purpose

1. **Review Your Early Work**

Look back at your Day 1 notes, sketches, or photos. Compare your first attempts with your latest work. What differences do you see in quality, style, or confidence?

2. List Your Learned Skills

Write down everything you've learned—quilting techniques, sneaker construction, creative planning, photography, community building, etc. You might be surprised how much ground you've covered.

3. Identify Your Breakthrough Moments

Think about the turning points in your journey—when something "clicked," a challenge you overcame, or a project you were especially proud of. These moments define your growth more than any single design.

4. Acknowledge Challenges and Wins

Note what was difficult, frustrating, or surprising—and how you responded. Recognize the resilience and problem-solving that got you here.

5. Write a Short Reflection Letter to Yourself

In a paragraph or two, write a note to your "Day 1 self." Encourage, congratulate, and remind yourself of how far you've come. Keep it to reread anytime you need a boost.

B. Why This Matters

Reflection turns practice into progress. It helps you see your journey clearly, recognize your evolution, and gain a deeper appreciation for your effort. By looking back, you build clarity and confidence for the road ahead.

C. Tips & Creative Ideas

- **Create a Visual Timeline**: Arrange photos from each week of the journey to see your growth.

- **Record a Voice Note or Video**: Speak your reflections out loud—it makes it more personal and powerful.

- **Use a Prompt Journal**: Answer questions like: "What surprised me?" "What am I most proud of?" "What did I enjoy the most?"

- **Make a Highlights Collage**: Combine your favorite photos and quotes from your journey so far.

D. Reflection & Motivation

Today, you gave yourself the gift of perspective. Reflection isn't just about the past—it's fuel for the future. You've grown in skill, mindset, and creative courage—and the best part is, this is only the beginning. Tomorrow, you'll take that progress and turn it into a celebration of your accomplishments. You've earned it—be proud.

Day 41: Celebrate Your Quilted Sneaker Achievements

You've accomplished something truly special. Today is a day of celebration—a moment to step back, admire your work, and recognize just how far you've come. From the first cut of fabric to the final stitch and the creative risks along the way, you've turned ideas into wearable art. That deserves to be celebrated with pride and joy.

Acknowledging your achievements builds momentum. It reminds you that the time, effort, and creativity you invested were worth it—and that you're capable of even more.

Take a moment to honor your hard work and the unique pieces you've created.

A. Step-by-Step Lesson: Mark This Creative Milestone

1. Display Your Favorite Pair

Put your quilted sneakers on display—on a shelf, a stand, or even in a shadowbox. Treat them like the artwork they are. Seeing them daily will remind you of your journey and success.

2. Share Your "Win" with Others

Post a photo, video, or story about your accomplishment. Share it with your online community, family, or friends. Let them cheer you on and celebrate with you.

3. Create a Project Recap Page

Write or design a single-page "recap" with photos, favorite moments, and lessons learned. Include details like your favorite pattern, fabric, or theme from your series.

4. Do Something Special to Celebrate

Treat yourself in a way that feels meaningful—wear your sneakers out for the first time, host a mini celebration, or do a creative photoshoot. Let this moment feel as big as it is.

5. Give Gratitude to Your Creative Self

Thank yourself for showing up, pushing through, and daring to try something new. Your creative self deserves recognition and care.

B. Why This Matters

Celebration is how we anchor progress. It honors your commitment and creativity, builds confidence, and makes the experience joyful and memorable. Taking time to celebrate fuels your desire to keep going—not just with sneakers, but with any creative pursuit you choose next.

C. Tips & Creative Ideas

- **Host a Virtual Reveal**: Share your final sneakers in a livestream or video countdown.

- **Create a Custom Sneaker Tag**: Make a small tag or card that documents the title, date, and inspiration for your finished pair.

- **Name Your Favorite Pair**: Give them an official name like an artist would name a painting.

- **Make a "Next Step" Wall**: Put up your sneakers with a note about what they inspired you to do next.

D. Reflection & Motivation

Today you paused to celebrate—and that matters more than you know. You've proven that you can commit, create, and complete something unique and powerful. This journey has been about much more than fabric and stitching—it's been about expression, learning, and growth. Tomorrow, you'll set new creative goals to keep that momentum going. You've done something amazing—enjoy it fully.

Day 42: Set Future Quilted Sneaker Goals

After celebrating your achievements, it's time to look ahead. Today's focus is on setting clear, inspiring goals for your future as a quilted sneaker designer. Whether you want to keep creating for fun, start a business, or teach others, defining your next steps will keep your creativity moving forward with purpose and direction.

This isn't about pressure—it's about vision. Setting thoughtful goals helps you grow on your terms, at your pace, with excitement and intention.

Setting future goals keeps your momentum going and gives your creativity a clear direction.

A. Step-by-Step Lesson: Define What Comes Next

1. Reflect on What You Loved Most

Think back over the past 41 days. What part of the process lit you up? Was it design? Quilting? Customization? Sharing your work? Your favorite moments point the way toward your future goals.

2. Set 1–3 Creative Goals

Choose 1–3 specific, actionable goals based on where you want to go next. Examples:

- Make a new pair each season or holiday
- Launch a small product line or Etsy shop
- Collaborate with another artist or sneaker customizer
- Learn a new quilting technique or tool
- Teach a class or host a workshop

3. Break Goals into Mini Steps

For each big goal, outline the next 2–3 small actions. (Example: If your goal is to launch a product line, your first step might be designing 3 new pairs or researching small-batch manufacturing.)

4. Set a Timeline

Add gentle deadlines to keep yourself on track. Whether it's "by the end of the month" or "this year," setting a timeline adds clarity and keeps your goals from drifting.

5. Write Down and Post Your Goals

Put your goals somewhere visible—in your studio, notebook, or digital planner. Seeing them daily keeps you focused and motivated to take action.

B. Why This Matters

Creativity thrives on purpose. Setting future goals gives you direction, momentum, and a reason to keep showing up to your craft. With clear goals in place, your quilted sneaker journey doesn't end here—it evolves, grows, and gets even more exciting.

C. Tips & Creative Ideas

- **Create a Vision Board**: Use images, fabrics, words, and sketches that represent your next creative chapter.

- **Start a "Next Pair" Notebook**: Dedicate pages to new ideas, sketches, themes, or materials.

- **Track Progress Publicly**: Share your goals with your online community to stay accountable.

- **Reward Milestones**: Celebrate each small win as you complete steps toward your goals.

D. Reflection & Motivation

Today you committed to your creative future. You've come so far—and you've only just begun. The skills, confidence, and passion you've built will fuel your next chapter. Tomorrow, you'll focus on the secret to long-term success: staying consistent with your creative practice. Your journey is in motion, and it's yours to shape.

Day 43: Stay Consistent With Your Creative Practice

Today's focus is one of the most important keys to long-term success: **creative consistency**. Inspiration will come and go, but building a steady, sustainable practice ensures you keep growing—regardless of mood, motivation, or life's busyness. Staying consistent doesn't mean doing something big every day. It means showing up regularly in ways that keep your creativity alive and progressing.

The goal isn't perfection—it's momentum.

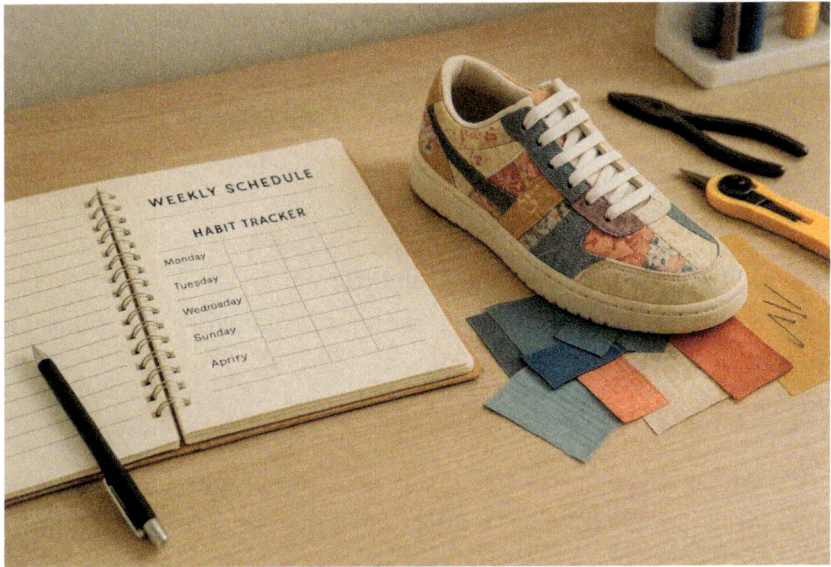

Staying consistent with small, regular creative sessions leads to big breakthroughs over time.

A. Step-by-Step Lesson: Build Your Creative Rhythm

1. Define Your Creative Frequency

Choose a pace that feels realistic and sustainable. For example:

- o Quilt sneakers once a week

- o Sketch or brainstorm new ideas every Sunday

- o Work on a small part of a project for 30 minutes, 2–3 times per week
  Consistency works best when it fits your life—not fights it.

2. Create a Dedicated Creative Space or Ritual

Set up a small workspace, even if it's temporary, where you can work comfortably. Pair your practice with a positive ritual like making tea, playing music, or lighting a candle to signal it's creative time.

3. **Track Progress, Not Perfection**

Use a journal, calendar, or app to mark your creative check-ins. Focus on showing up—not finishing something perfect every time. Each effort adds up over time.

4. **Mix It Up When Needed**

To avoid burnout, alternate between different creative activities: designing, stitching, planning, or even just organizing materials. The key is staying engaged, not stuck.

5. **Allow Grace for Off Days**

Life happens. If you miss a day or a week, don't quit—just pick back up where you left off. What matters most is your ability to return to the practice when you're ready.

B. Why This Matters

Consistency builds confidence, skill, and creative identity. It helps you improve over time, develop a strong personal style, and bring more joy and purpose into your daily life. It's how great projects—and great artists—are made.

C. Tips & Creative Ideas

- **Use a Creative Tracker**: Check off each creative day or task in a visual way.

- **Set Monthly Mini-Challenges**: Give yourself a fun prompt or goal each month.

- **Join a Maker's Group or Accountability Buddy**: Share your weekly progress with someone else.

- **Rotate Between "Fun" and "Focus" Projects**: Keep things both playful and purposeful.

D. Reflection & Motivation

Today you made a powerful choice: to stay creatively active, not just when it's easy—but as a lifestyle. This decision will carry your work further than talent or trends ever could. You're not just a hobbyist—you're a consistent, dedicated creator. Next, we'll dive into the final chapter of your journey—turning your passion into lasting impact, joy, and legacy. Keep showing up—you're becoming unstoppable.

Chapter 14 Review: E – Embrace Your Quilting Journey

Chapter 14 covered **Days 40–43** of your journey through the 50-Day **Q-U-I-L-T-I-N-G S-N-E-A-K-E-R-S** system, focusing on **E – Embrace Your Quilting Journey**. This chapter helped you reflect on your progress, celebrate your accomplishments, and set future goals. You learned the importance of recognizing how far you've come, staying motivated, and maintaining consistency in your creative practice.

Day 40 – Reflect on Your Progress and Growth

- **Review your creative journey** – Reflect on what you've learned and how your skills have improved over the last 40 days.

- **Celebrate your growth** – Take note of the challenges you've overcome and the progress you've made as a maker.

- **Identify strengths** – Recognize the areas where you've gained confidence and the techniques you now excel in.

- **Acknowledge your effort** – Take a moment to appreciate the time, energy, and passion you've invested in your craft.

Day 41 – Celebrate Your Quilted Sneaker Achievements

- **Honor your accomplishments** – Celebrate the completion of your first pair (or several pairs) of quilted sneakers.

- **Share your success** – Show off your work on social media, tell your story, and invite others to join in your excitement.

- **Take pride in your creations** – Whether you're gifting, selling, or keeping your sneakers, be proud of what you've made.

- **Create a sense of closure** – Let this moment feel like a milestone, a time to look back at everything you've achieved so far.

Day 42 – Set Future Quilted Sneaker Goals

- **Clarify what's next** – Identify new challenges or projects you want to take on.

- **Set actionable, inspiring goals** – Whether it's creating a new design, launching a collection, or teaching others, define where you want your quilting journey to go.

- **Create a plan of action** – Break down your goals into manageable steps and timelines.

- **Stay flexible** – Your creative goals can evolve as you grow, so allow room for new opportunities to come your way.

Day 43 – Stay Consistent With Your Creative Practice

- **Establish a routine** – Commit to regular creative sessions to maintain momentum.

- **Set aside time for creativity** – Schedule time each week for quilting, whether it's for fun or focused projects.

- **Track your progress** – Keep a journal or creative log of what you're working on, any breakthroughs, or new techniques you're exploring.

- **Be patient and persistent** – Understand that consistency leads to growth, even on days when inspiration feels low.

By the end of Chapter 14, you've reflected on your journey, celebrated your achievements, and set new intentions for the future. In **Chapter 15: R – Reach New Heights in Sneaker Quilting (Days 44–47)**, you'll learn how to take your creative practice even further—turning passion into profit, launching new projects, and building a lasting legacy with your quilted sneakers.

Chapter 15: R – Reach New Heights in Sneaker Quilting

Chapter 15 focuses on **R** for **Reach New Heights in Sneaker Quilting**, a transformative section of the **50-day Q-U-I-L-T-I-N-G S-N-E-A-K-E.R.S. System**. In **Day 44**, you'll learn how to turn your newfound passion for quilted sneakers into a potential source of income or a rewarding hobby. Whether you're interested in selling your creations or simply continuing to develop your craft, this day helps set you on the path to monetizing or deepening your involvement in the quilting community. **Day 45** explores the options for selling or gifting your quilted sneakers, encouraging you to share your art with the world. **Day 46** inspires you to plan future quilting adventures—whether through new techniques, collections, or collaborations—taking your skills beyond the basics and into exciting new projects. Finally, **Day 47** helps you reflect on how to build a personal quilting legacy, ensuring your work is remembered and valued by others. This chapter is about amplifying your craft and making lasting connections, both creatively and professionally.

Take your creative passion to the next level by turning it into a product, gift, or brand.

Day 44: Turn Passion into Profit or a Rewarding Hobby

You've built an incredible creative skill—now it's time to explore what comes next. Today's focus is helping you decide how you want quilted sneakers to fit into your life long-term. Whether you turn it into a profitable side hustle or keep it as a passion-fueled hobby, the path you choose should align with your values, goals, and lifestyle.

This step is about defining success on your own terms—and building a path that brings joy, growth, and fulfillment.

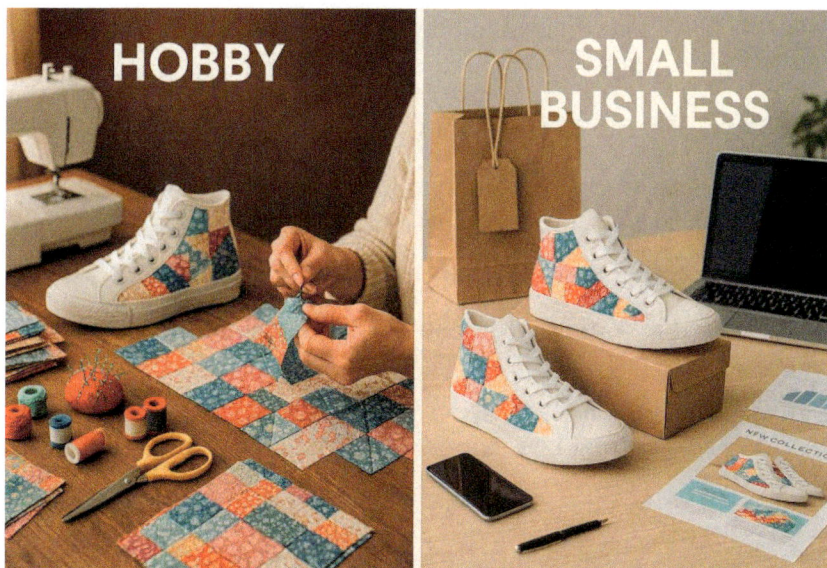

Whether it's for joy or income, quilting sneakers can be a fulfilling part of your lifestyle.

A. Step-by-Step Lesson: Choose Your Creative Path

1. Clarify Your Purpose Moving Forward

Ask yourself:

- o Do I want to build a brand or business from this?

- o Do I want to create for fun, for gifts, or personal satisfaction?

- o Do I want to teach or inspire others?
  Knowing your "why" helps guide your time, energy, and decisions.

2. Explore Hobby vs. Business Options

- o **Hobby**: Make sneakers for yourself, friends, art shows, or just creative joy.

- o **Profit Path**: Create a small batch shop, take custom orders, or sell digital templates or classes.
  You can switch between the two anytime—it's your journey.

3. Assess Time & Resources

Determine how much time and budget you realistically want to commit. This helps you avoid burnout and stay focused, especially if you're considering selling or teaching.

4. Test the Waters with Low-Risk Experiments

Try one small step, such as:

- o Selling one pair on Etsy or at a craft fair

- o Teaching a one-hour workshop

- o Offering a giveaway in exchange for feedback
  Let the response guide your next move.

5. Set Boundaries and Keep It Fun

Whether hobby or business, protect your joy. Set clear boundaries, build at your own pace, and stay connected to the creative spark that got you started.

B. Why This Matters

You've invested time, energy, and love into this journey—and now you get to decide what it becomes. Choosing your direction with intention means your quilted sneaker practice will continue to support, uplift, and energize you in the long term.

C. Tips & Creative Ideas

- **Start a Side Project Name or Brand**: Even for fun, naming your work helps create identity.

- **Create a Pricing Guide**: If selling, calculate time, materials, and labor fairly.

- **Keep a Passion Folder**: Save ideas and inspiration that are just for you—purely creative.

- **Check In Regularly**: Revisit your goals every few months and adjust your path as needed.

D. Reflection & Motivation

Today you made a powerful decision: to shape your creative future around what matters most to you. Whether your quilted sneakers remain a personal joy or grow into something more, this craft is now a permanent part of who you are. Tomorrow, we'll explore how to share that joy even further—through gifting, selling, and spreading your creations into the world. You're ready for the next level—your way.

Day 45: Sell or Gift Your Quilted Sneakers

You've created something personal, beautiful, and truly one of a kind—now it's time to share it. Today's focus is on how to **sell or**

gift your quilted sneakers with care and purpose. Whether you're making someone's day with a handmade gift or testing the waters as a creative entrepreneur, this step is about sharing your art in meaningful, impactful ways.

Giving or selling your sneakers turns your creation into a story someone else can wear, love, and appreciate. That's a powerful extension of your creativity.

Share your art with others through sales, gifts, or custom orders that spread joy and value.

A. Step-by-Step Lesson: Share Your Sneakers with the World

1. Decide the Intention Behind the Share

Ask yourself:

- o Is this pair meant for a loved one, a first customer, or a showcase piece?

- Do I want to build a business or just share my work with others in small ways?
  Knowing the purpose helps you package and present your sneakers meaningfully.

2. Gifting: Make It Personal

If gifting, consider including:

- A handwritten note about the inspiration or meaning behind the pair

- A care card with cleaning instructions

- A custom bag or box for a polished presentation
  Giving your creation as a gift turns it into a memory.

3. Selling: Start Small and Smart

If selling, choose a beginner-friendly platform like Etsy, Depop, or Instagram Shops.

- Take clean, clear photos (Day 31!)

- Write honest descriptions of materials, fit, and care

- Price based on time, materials, and value—not just comparison

4. Ensure Proper Fit and Finish

Whether gifting or selling, make sure:

- The sneakers are clean and protected

- Stitching is tight and embellishments are secure

- Presentation reflects the care you put into making them

5. Ask for Feedback or a Photo

Whether from a buyer or a gift recipient, ask if they'll share a photo of the sneakers in action. Seeing your work appreciated in real life is incredibly rewarding—and can help promote future designs.

B. Why This Matters

Selling or gifting your sneakers completes the creative cycle—it's the moment your work leaves your hands and becomes part of someone else's world. It brings meaning to your process and shows the real value of handmade craftsmanship.

C. Tips & Creative Ideas

- **Offer Limited Drops**: Sell one pair at a time with a "first come, first served" model.

- **Create a "Gift Edition" Design**: Make a special version just for birthdays, holidays, or milestones.

- **Include a Creative Story Card**: Explain the name, inspiration, or details of the design.

- **Ask for a Testimonial**: If selling, positive reviews build trust for future customers.

D. Reflection & Motivation

Today, you gave your creativity a new life—beyond your own shelf or studio. Whether as a heartfelt gift or a small business step, sharing your quilted sneakers is an act of generosity and confidence. Tomorrow, you'll build on this momentum by planning your next creative adventure. You've made something worth celebrating—and now, you've shared it.

Day 46: Plan Future Quilting Adventures

With so many skills under your belt, it's time to dream big again. Today is all about **planning your future quilting adventures**— projects, experiences, and creative challenges that excite and energize you. You've already proven you can design, build, and finish a pair of custom quilted sneakers. Now, the question is: Where do you want your creativity to take you next?

Planning ahead helps you stay inspired, organized, and aligned with your goals—while leaving room for exploration and fun.

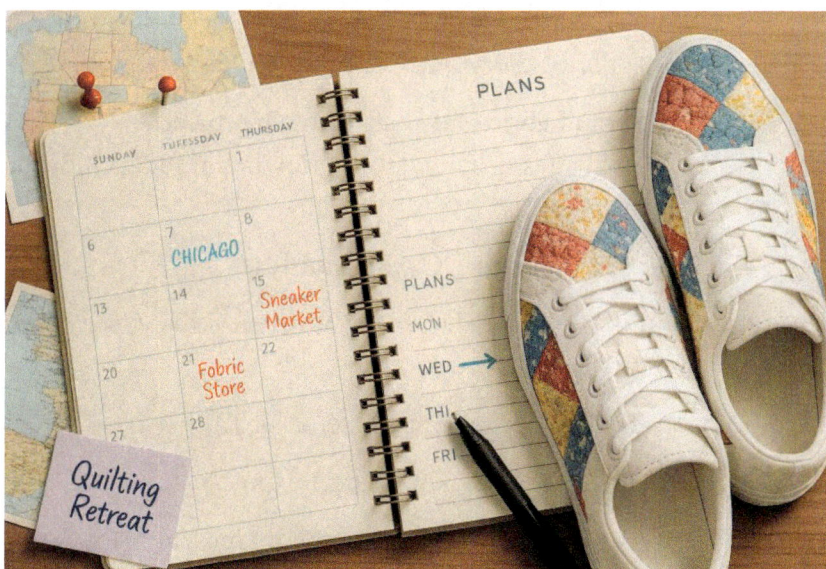

Plan events, collaborations, or travel that aligns with your sneaker quilting passion.

A. Step-by-Step Lesson: Map Out What's Next

1. Start a Quilted Sneaker Bucket List

Write down exciting project ideas or goals you haven't tried yet. Examples:

- o Quilt a matching sneaker-and-bag combo

- o Try quilting with metallic or recycled fabrics

- o Make a themed pair for a holiday, concert, or event

- o Design a sneaker inspired by your heritage or personal story

2. Plan a Creative Challenge

Design your own 7-day, 14-day, or monthly mini project. Challenge ideas:

- o "One Panel a Day" quilting series

- o "Color of the Month" sneaker builds

- o "Scrap Fabric Only" sustainable project
  Challenges keep creativity flowing in fun, achievable ways.

3. Explore New Learning Opportunities

Identify any quilting, sewing, design, or business skills you'd like to grow. You might try:

- o Taking a new class (online or local)

- o Attending a sneaker or craft expo

- o Visiting fabric markets or textile museums for inspiration

4. Set a Dream Project

Define one big creative project that excites you—like launching your own small sneaker collection, hosting a workshop, or submitting your work to an art show. Even if it feels far away, write it down.

5. Make a Timeline or Mood Board

Visualize your goals by creating a roadmap, digital vision board, or sketchbook plan. This gives structure and motivation to turn future ideas into reality.

B. Why This Matters

Quilting adventures keep your passion alive and evolving. When you intentionally plan what's next, you're investing in yourself as an artist and honoring your creative momentum. It also gives you something exciting to look forward to—even after this 50-day journey ends.

C. Tips & Creative Ideas

- **Use a Dedicated Notebook**: Keep track of new fabrics, themes, sketches, and ideas.

- **Connect with Other Creators**: Collaborate on a future sneaker project or trade materials.

- **Explore New Materials**: Try quilting with denim, silk, mesh, or vinyl for different effects.

- **Set a Fun Reward**: Treat yourself after each major milestone or project completed.

D. Reflection & Motivation

Today you took charge of your creative future. Planning your next quilting adventure keeps the fire alive and your ideas flowing. You're no longer following a system—you're leading your own path. Tomorrow, we'll focus on how to build a lasting legacy with your creativity. The journey doesn't end here—it expands.

Day 47: Build Your Personal Quilting Legacy

You've created, shared, taught, and planned ahead—now it's time to think long-term. Today's focus is on building your **personal quilting legacy**. A legacy isn't about fame or followers—it's about leaving something meaningful behind. It's about how your creativity, voice, and work can inspire others, tell your story, and live on in your own unique way.

Your quilted sneakers are more than projects—they're pieces of your journey, stitched with purpose and personality. Let's look at how to preserve, document, and grow your legacy for years to come.

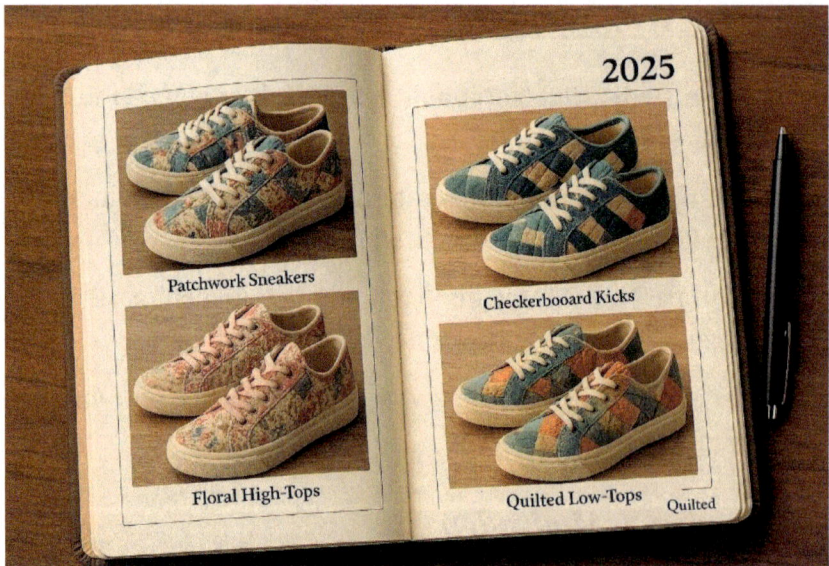

Document your journey to leave a creative legacy others can learn from and celebrate.

A. Step-by-Step Lesson: Define & Preserve Your Legacy

1. Clarify What You Want to Be Known For

Ask yourself:

- What style, message, or value do I bring to my designs?
- What makes my sneakers "me"?
- What do I want people to feel when they see or wear my work?
  Your legacy starts with knowing your creative identity.

2. Document Your Process and Growth

Organize photos, sketches, notes, and reflections into a digital archive or physical portfolio. Label dates, design names, and milestones. This becomes a timeline of your evolution and creative voice.

3. Create a Signature Style or Series

Develop a recognizable thread across your work—whether it's through color, stitching style, storytelling, or materials. Consistency builds your identity and gives your work lasting recognition.

4. Pass It On

Share your knowledge through tutorials, workshops, or mentoring. Consider writing a blog, zine, or even a book. Legacy is built by helping others begin their own creative journeys.

5. Preserve a Piece for the Future

Choose a favorite pair of sneakers and store them as part of your creative archive. Add a tag with the date, title, and a note about its significance. One day, it could inspire future generations—or your future self.

B. Why This Matters

A legacy reflects who you are and what you've created with love, time, and care. By thinking intentionally about your creative footprint, you transform everyday projects into something lasting. It's not about perfection—it's about purpose.

C. Tips & Creative Ideas

- **Create a Digital Lookbook or Website**: Showcase your full body of work in one beautiful place.

- **Make a "Legacy Sneaker"**: Design one pair that represents your full journey so far.

- **Build a Maker's Journal**: Include sketches, fabric swatches, photos, quotes, and memories.

- **Write a Creative Manifesto**: Describe what quilting sneakers means to you in your own words.

D. Reflection & Motivation

Today, you looked beyond the present and into the future of your creative story. Your quilted sneaker journey is now part of something greater—your voice, your passion, and your influence. Whether you continue making for years or take a break and return later, your work matters. Your legacy is already being built, one stitch, one pair, one story at a time.

Chapter 15 Review: R – Reach New Heights in Sneaker Quilting

Chapter 15 covered **Days 44–47** of your journey through the 50-Day **Q-U-I-L-T-I-N-G S-N-E-A-K-E-R-S** system, focusing on **R – Reach New Heights in Sneaker Quilting**. This chapter explored how to take your quilted sneaker creations to the next level, whether you want to turn your passion into a profitable business, gift your designs to others, or plan your long-term creative path.

Day 44 – Turn Passion into Profit or a Rewarding Hobby

- **Decide on your approach** – Choose whether you want to build a business or keep quilting sneakers as a personal hobby.

- **Define your goals** – If you're pursuing profit, think about starting small with custom orders or selling online. If you want to keep it a hobby, focus on enjoyment, personal expression, and gifting.

- **Balance your passion and practicality** – Know how much time, energy, and money you're willing to invest, and set realistic expectations.

- **Set clear intentions** – Whether making money or honing your craft, create goals that align with your creative vision and lifestyle.

Day 45 – Sell or Gift Your Quilted Sneakers

- **Choose your selling platform** – Decide whether to sell on Etsy, Instagram, or at local craft fairs.

- **Market your creations** – Use high-quality photos and a clear description of your designs, materials, and customization options.

- **Gift with intention** – If gifting, make the process personal by adding a note or customizing the sneakers to the recipient's taste.

- **Consider limited-edition releases** – Create exclusivity by offering a small batch or custom pairs that enhance the value of your work.

Day 46 – Plan Future Quilting Adventures

- **Expand your creative horizons** – Look beyond sneakers and think about new projects like bags, jackets, or home décor using quilting techniques.

- **Take on more complex challenges** – Push your design skills by trying new techniques or larger collections.

- **Build a timeline** – Plan out what you want to work on in the next few months or year, setting short- and long-term goals for your creative projects.

- **Explore new materials or partnerships** – Try out different fabrics, collaborate with other creators, or experiment with mixed media in your next projects.

Day 47 – Build Your Personal Quilting Legacy

- **Define your creative legacy** – Reflect on how you want your work to be remembered. Think about the style, techniques, and personal stories you've incorporated into your designs.

- **Create a signature look** – Establish a recognizable design or theme that people associate with your work.

- **Share your knowledge** – Pass on your skills by teaching others, writing about your journey, or documenting your process for future generations.

- **Celebrate your progress** – Every pair of quilted sneakers you create is part of your growing legacy, whether you make a few or thousands.

By the end of Chapter 15, you've taken significant steps toward establishing your creative practice as both an art and a potential business. In **Chapter 16: S – Sustain & Scale Your Success (Days 48–50)**, you'll learn how to grow your quilting sneaker brand, launch new products, and become a lifelong expert in your craft. You're ready for your next big step—let's take it!

Chapter 16: S – Sustain & Scale Your Success

Chapter 16 represents **S** for **Sustain & Scale Your Success** within the **50-day Q-U-I-L-T-I-N-G S-N-E-A-K-E-R-S System**. In **Day 48**, you'll learn how to grow your quilted sneaker brand, taking the foundations you've built over the past 47 days and expanding them into a recognizable, sustainable venture. This day helps you focus on growing your presence, whether online or in person, to reach a broader audience. **Day 49** dives into the importance of launching a signature product or collection, allowing you to make a bold statement with a cohesive set of designs that reflect your unique style and artistic vision. Finally, **Day 50** is about solidifying your status as a lifelong quilted sneaker expert, ensuring that you continue to evolve, innovate, and inspire others within the quilting and sneaker communities. This chapter is the culmination of your creative journey, setting you up for long-term success and continued passion in your craft.

Scaling your success means thinking long-term—build systems, style, and visibility.

Day 48: Grow Your Quilted Sneaker Brand

You've created a body of work that reflects passion, style, and skill—now it's time to **grow your brand** around it. Whether you want to build a small creative business, grow an online presence, or simply establish a recognizable identity, today is about turning your personal creativity into something that reaches and resonates with others.

A strong brand doesn't mean going corporate. It means crafting a consistent, authentic image and message that represents who you are and what your work stands for.

Define a clear visual identity and message that reflects your values and creative vibe.

A. Step-by-Step Lesson: Build Your Creative Brand

1. **Define Your Brand Identity**

Answer these questions:

- o What 3 words describe my quilted sneaker style?
- o What values or themes appear in my designs (e.g., bold, nostalgic, eco-conscious)?
- o What feeling do I want people to associate with my creations?

  Your answers will shape your brand voice, visual style, and storytelling.

2. Choose a Brand Name or Signature

Create a name for your sneaker work—even if it's just for fun or informal use. You can use your name, a phrase, or something symbolic that reflects your style. This adds professionalism and makes your work easier to find and share.

3. Design a Visual Style

Choose 2–3 brand colors, fonts, or visual elements you'll use in photos, packaging, or your online presence. Consistency in these areas helps people instantly recognize your work.

4. Build or Improve Your Online Presence

Update your social media bio, portfolio, or website to reflect your branding. Include a short statement about who you are, what you make, and how people can connect with or support your work.

5. Engage with Your Audience

Post consistently, share behind-the-scenes process shots, and invite conversation. Respond to comments and DMs with authenticity. A great brand is more than visuals—it's about connection.

B. Why This Matters

Branding gives your work identity, clarity, and direction. It helps you stand out, attract the right audience, and grow your reach while staying true to your voice. A strong brand makes it easier to share your creativity in meaningful, memorable ways.

C. Tips & Creative Ideas

- **Create a Sneaker Tag or Label**: Add a fabric tag or card with your brand name to each pair.

- **Use Templates for Posts**: Design Canva or Photoshop templates to make posting easier and more polished.

- **Create a "Brand Board"**: Keep swatches, logos, colors, and voice guidelines in one place for consistency.

- **Tell Your Story Often**: Let people in on your "why"—your story is part of your brand.

D. Reflection & Motivation

Today you gave your creativity a clear identity. You're not just making sneakers—you're building something lasting, recognizable, and uniquely yours. Branding gives your talent a voice that others can follow, support, and celebrate. Tomorrow, you'll take the next bold step: launching a signature product or collection to showcase the heart of your creative brand. You're ready to be seen—and remembered.

Day 49: Launch a Signature Product or Collection

You've built your brand, refined your craft, and developed your creative voice—now it's time to **launch your signature product or collection**. This is your moment to take everything you've created and package it into a showcase offering that represents your style, story, and skill. Whether it's a single standout pair, a themed series, or a matching accessory set, this launch is your creative debut to the world.

Today is about making your work official—and unforgettable.

Create a signature collection to establish your niche and build anticipation with your audience.

A. Step-by-Step Lesson: Bring Your Signature Offering to Life

1. Choose What to Launch

Your signature offering should reflect your best work and your unique style. Examples:

- One fully finished, named pair of quilted sneakers
- A 3–5 pair collection based on a theme (seasons, emotions, art, etc.)
- A sneaker + accessory combo set (with matching pouch or keychain)

    o A limited drop of made-to-order custom designs

2. Name and Package the Product or Series

Give it a title that captures the essence of the design or collection. Include a short story or tagline. Create a thoughtful presentation—add tags, tissue paper, or a care card. Details add polish and professionalism.

3. Photograph and Promote Your Work

Use your photos from earlier days (or shoot fresh ones!) to capture your work beautifully. Post a countdown or teaser to build interest. Then, reveal the product with a launch post across your platforms.

4. Choose Your Platform and Price Point

Sell directly on Instagram, through Etsy, or via your own site. If you're not selling, showcase the launch like an art reveal—celebrate it as a creative milestone. Set prices that reflect your time, materials, and value.

5. Celebrate and Collect Feedback

When you launch, celebrate! Share the meaning behind your work, thank your followers, and ask for feedback or testimonials. Every interaction is a chance to grow your creative presence.

B. Why This Matters

Launching a signature product or collection establishes you as a creator with vision and intention. It gives you a tangible offering to share with the world and opens the door to recognition, opportunity, and potential growth. It's the next level of owning your artistry.

C. Tips & Creative Ideas

- **Use a Countdown or Behind-the-Scenes Series** to build excitement before your launch

- **Offer a Launch Bonus**: Add a small surprise for the first few customers or viewers

- **Host a Live or Premiere Reveal**: Go live or schedule a video to make your launch feel like an event

- **Keep It Exclusive**: Limit quantities or make it available only for a short time to build buzz

D. Reflection & Motivation

Today, you turned your creativity into a signature expression of who you are. Your launch represents more than a product—it's the story of your growth, your passion, and your power as a maker. Tomorrow, you'll close the loop by embracing this practice as a lifelong path. Your brand is born. Your work is out in the world. And this is only the beginning.

Day 50: Become a Lifelong Quilted Sneaker Expert

You've made it—**Day 50** of your creative journey. Today's focus is all about what comes next: fully stepping into your identity as a **lifelong quilted sneaker expert**. You've mastered the skills, built your confidence, and launched your work into the world. Now, it's time to embrace this craft as an ongoing part of who you are.

Being an expert doesn't mean knowing everything—it means continuing to learn, explore, and inspire others while staying deeply connected to your passion.

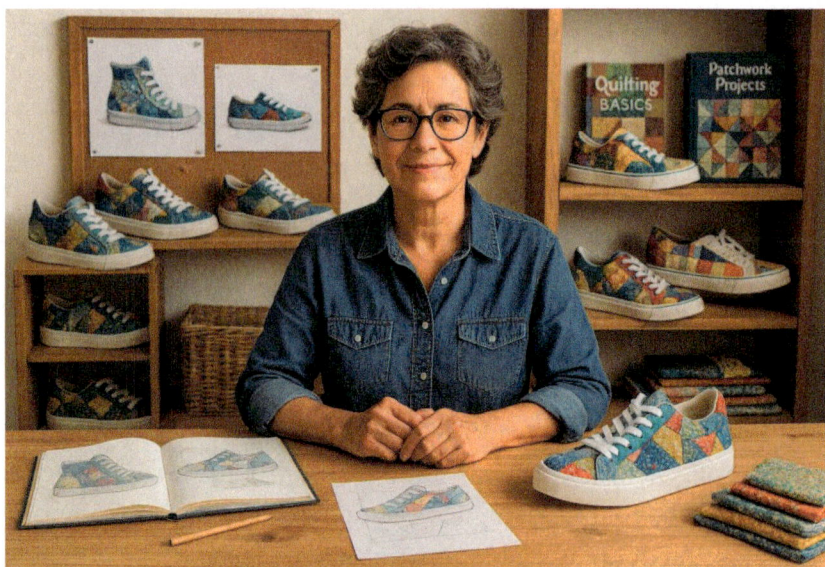

Mastery is a journey—keep learning, evolving, and inspiring others with your passion.

A. Step-by-Step Lesson: Step Into Your Creative Identity

1. Own Your Expertise

Reflect on everything you've learned: from tools and techniques to storytelling, branding, and sharing your work. You are no longer a beginner—you're a designer, a maker, and a voice in the creative community.

2. Commit to Lifelong Learning

Keep evolving. Explore new quilting styles, sneaker designs, or even materials you've never tried. Stay curious. Attend workshops, learn from other makers, or experiment with bold, unconventional ideas.

3. Teach, Mentor, or Lead

Share your experience with others. Create tutorials, mentor beginners, or host creative meetups. You don't need a big following—just a willingness to help someone else take their first step.

4. Build a Body of Work Over Time

Continue creating and documenting. With each new pair, collection, or project, your portfolio will grow—and so will your legacy. Aim to make work you're proud of, not just popular.

5. Keep the Joy Alive

Most importantly, never lose the spark. Make time for fun, play, and passion projects. Celebrate milestones, take breaks when needed, and always come back to the reasons you started.

B. Why This Matters

Becoming a lifelong expert means embracing your creative identity with confidence and joy. It means choosing to stay committed to your craft—not just for the outcomes, but for the love of the process itself. It means leading by example, inspiring others, and continuing to grow no matter where life takes you.

C. Tips & Creative Ideas

- **Create an Annual Sneaker Series**: Make one signature pair each year that captures where you are creatively

- **Keep a "Mastermaker" Journal**: Record insights, goals, new techniques, and evolving ideas

- **Give Back to the Community**: Donate a pair, collaborate with a student, or host a free class

- **Celebrate Your Journey**: Revisit Day 1 every year and reflect on how far you've come

D. Reflection & Motivation

Today, you crossed the finish line—and stepped into a new beginning. You've become a quilted sneaker expert not by title, but by effort, passion, and persistence. You've stitched together a story of creativity, courage, and growth. And now, you carry that forward—not just as a craft, but as a calling.

Your journey doesn't end here—it evolves. You are the designer, the maker, and the mentor. Keep creating. Keep sharing. Keep walking your path—one custom pair at a time.

Chapter 16 Review: S – Sustain & Scale Your Success

Chapter 16 covered **Days 48–50** of your journey through the 50-Day **Q-U-I-L-T-I-N-G S-N-E-A-K-E-R-S** system, focusing on **S – Sustain & Scale Your Success**. This chapter provided the tools and strategies to expand your quilted sneaker practice from a personal project to a thriving brand. It's all about scaling your creations, creating signature products, and positioning yourself as an expert in the field.

Day 48 – Grow Your Quilted Sneaker Brand

- **Build your brand identity** – Continue to refine your brand's voice, visual style, and message to resonate with your target audience.

- **Expand your online presence** – Use social media, your website, and online marketplaces to reach a broader audience.

- **Leverage customer relationships** – Build loyal followers by connecting with your audience, encouraging engagement, and sharing behind-the-scenes content.

- **Collaborate with influencers or artists** – Partner with individuals who align with your brand to expand your reach and increase credibility.

Day 49 – Launch a Signature Product or Collection

- **Create a cohesive product line** – Develop a collection or signature product that reflects your unique style, whether it's a limited-edition sneaker design, a seasonal collection, or a themed release.

- **Market your collection** – Use storytelling, photography, and social media to create buzz and anticipation before your launch.

- **Focus on presentation** – From packaging to product descriptions, ensure that your collection is presented professionally and consistently.

- **Encourage exclusivity** – Offer limited releases or pre-orders to make your product feel special and desirable.

Day 50 – Become a Lifelong Quilted Sneaker Expert

- **Commit to continuous learning** – Keep developing your skills by exploring new techniques, materials, and design trends.

- **Share your expertise** – Position yourself as an expert by teaching others, writing articles, or creating tutorials.

- **Track your growth** – Look back at your journey and assess how much you've learned and achieved, setting new goals for the future.

- **Stay passionate and inspired** – Never lose sight of why you started quilting sneakers—your creativity and dedication will keep you moving forward.

By the end of Chapter 16, you've built a sustainable foundation for your creative practice. You've learned how to grow your brand, launch professional collections, and position yourself as a leader in the quilted sneaker community. Your journey doesn't end here; in fact, it's just the beginning. You are now equipped with the skills, knowledge, and vision to scale your success and become a lifelong expert in quilted sneaker design.

Conclusion

As you wrap up your 50-day Quilted Sneaker Journey, take pride in the skills you've developed and the creativity you've unleashed. From the very first step of understanding the basics to the final stitch of your custom design, you've successfully navigated the **Q-U-I-L-T-I-N-G S-N-E-A-K-E-R-S System**, building confidence and mastery each day. You've learned how to select the right materials, create intricate patterns, apply advanced techniques, and put your personal stamp on every detail. Completing this journey not only results in your very own handmade quilted sneakers but also opens the door to endless future possibilities, whether that means sharing your creations, launching a brand, or continuing to experiment and innovate. As you move forward, remember that the creativity you've cultivated here can be applied to countless other projects. Your journey doesn't end with this book—it's just the beginning of your path as a skilled, inspired sneaker artist. Keep the momentum going and enjoy every step of your quilting adventure!

Reflect on your full journey from beginner to confident sneaker quilter—one stitch at a time.

I. Recap of the 50-Day Quilted Sneaker Journey

Let's take one final walk through the full **Q-U-I-L-T-I-N-G S-N-E-A-K-E-R-S System** and the 50 steps that got you here:

- **Q – Quickstart Your Quilting Sneakers Journey (Days 1–3)**
  You discovered the art of quilted sneakers, set your creative goals, and built an inspiration board to kick off your journey.

- **U – Understand Essential Materials & Tools (Days 4–6)**
  You selected the right fabrics, chose your ideal sneaker base, and gathered the essential quilting tools for the job.

- **I – Inspire Your Quilted Sneaker Design (Days 7–9)**
  You explored quilt patterns, sketched your sneaker designs, and finalized a plan to guide your build.

- **L – Layout & Pattern Preparation (Days 10–12)**
  You measured your sneaker base, drafted pattern templates, and precisely cut your fabric to match.

- **T – Techniques for Quilting Sneakers (Days 13–15)**
  You practiced essential quilting stitches, tried out classic and modern quilting styles, and even explored advanced methods.

- **I – Integrate Quilted Panels onto Sneakers (Days 16–18)**
  You quilted your fabric panels, secured them to your sneakers, and perfected your stitching and assembly techniques.

- **N – Navigate Customizing & Detailing (Days 19–21)**
  You personalized your sneakers with embroidery, embellishments, and mixed media techniques that made your work truly unique.

- **G – Guarantee Professional-Level Finishing (Days 22–24)**
  You added clean edge finishes, sealed your project for protection, and completed a final round of quality checks.

- **S – Sustain & Maintain Quilted Sneakers (Days 25–27)**
  You learned how to clean, repair, and store your sneakers so they stay looking great for the long haul.

- **N – Next-Level Quilted Sneaker Techniques (Days 28–30)**
  You experimented with complex quilt patterns, incorporated other crafts, and innovated your own design approach.

- **E – Exhibit & Share Your Creations (Days 31–33)**
  You photographed your work, built a digital portfolio, and explored how to share your creations in public or online spaces.

- **A – Advance Your Sneaker Quilting Skills (Days 34–36)**
  You expanded your vision by creating matching accessories, trying advanced projects, and launching a themed collection.

- **K – Knowledge Sharing & Community (Days 37–39)**
  You connected with others, taught your craft, and began sharing your journey with the broader creative world.

- **E – Embrace Your Quilting Journey (Days 40–43)**
  You reflected on your progress, celebrated your wins, set new goals, and committed to consistency in your creative practice.

- **R – Reach New Heights in Sneaker Quilting (Days 44–47)**
  You explored selling, gifting, and planning future adventures—turning your passion into a rewarding pursuit or business.

- **S – Sustain & Scale Your Success (Days 48–50)**
  You grew your brand, developed a signature collection, and stepped fully into your role as a lifelong quilted sneaker expert.

II. Final Encouragement & What Comes Next

This isn't the end—it's a bold beginning.

You now have a powerful foundation, a full portfolio of skills, and a system you can return to again and again. Whether you continue quilting sneakers as a hobby, launch your own brand, or inspire others to try something creative, your work has meaning. It reflects your story, your voice, and your ability to make something entirely original.

Stay consistent. Stay curious. Keep pushing your creative boundaries.

And remember—every great pair of quilted sneakers begins with a single stitch. Keep stitching forward.

Appendices

The appendices section of *HowExpert Guide to Quilting Sneakers* serves as a valuable reference to support your creative journey. Here, you'll find essential resources to guide you through the quilting process and elevate your sneaker projects. From helpful patterns and templates to a complete guide of tools and suppliers, this section will make your experience even smoother. Additionally, we've included a troubleshooting and FAQ section to answer common questions, as well as a glossary of sneaker quilting terms for quick reference. For an extra burst of inspiration, you'll also find a quilted sneaker inspiration gallery to fuel your creativity. This comprehensive collection will be your go-to toolkit for the entire quilting sneaker experience.

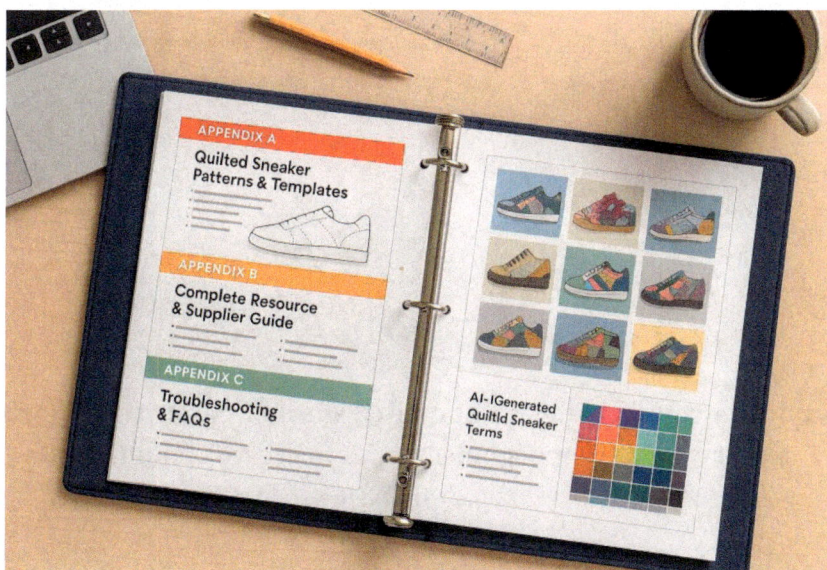

Use these bonus tools and templates to expand, troubleshoot, and enhance your sneaker quilting experience.

Appendix A: Quilted Sneaker Patterns & Templates

This section provides a comprehensive selection of patterns and templates to help you create flawless quilted sneakers. Whether you're a beginner or looking to perfect your quilting skills, these resources are designed to support your journey every step of the way. Each pattern comes with clear instructions, size guidelines, and color-coded sections to simplify the quilting process.

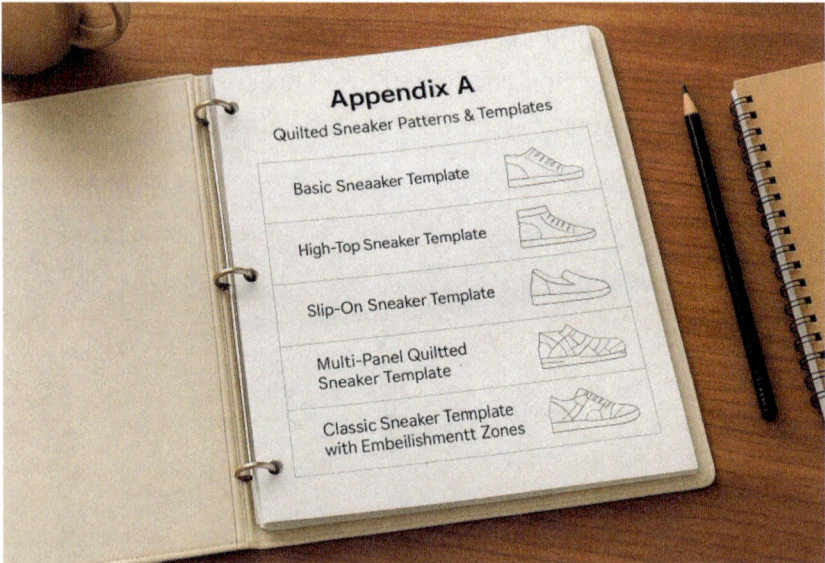

Explore a complete toolkit of quilted sneaker patterns—tailored to every style from beginner basics to creative, multi-panel designs.

~ ~ ~ ~ ~

A. Pattern Overview:

1. **Basic Sneaker Template**

- This pattern is ideal for beginners. It includes a basic, simple sneaker shape—perfect for experimenting with quilting techniques and materials.

- **Included:**

  - Full sneaker outline

  - Suggested fabric zones (upper, toe box, heel, etc.)

  - Marked stitching lines for basic quilting patterns (e.g., running stitch, diamond patterns)

  - A beginner-friendly approach to create your first quilted sneakers

- **Use for:** Any style, from canvas sneakers to simple slip-ons.

BASIC SNEAKER TEMPLATE

VAMP
UPPER
HEEL
TOE BOX
SOLE
FABRIC ZONES
STITCH LINES

Start your sneaker quilting journey with this beginner-friendly template featuring simple shapes and easy-to-follow stitch guides.

2. High-Top Sneaker Template

- Designed for high-top sneakers, this pattern features a taller upper that requires additional fabric shaping and quilting techniques.

- **Included:**

  - Detailed template with height and width measurements

  - Adjustments for the added ankle section

  - Stitched guide for multi-panel designs and creative finishes (e.g., geometric patterns)

- **Use for:** High-top sneakers with additional design elements such as extra fabric, embellishments, or layered designs.

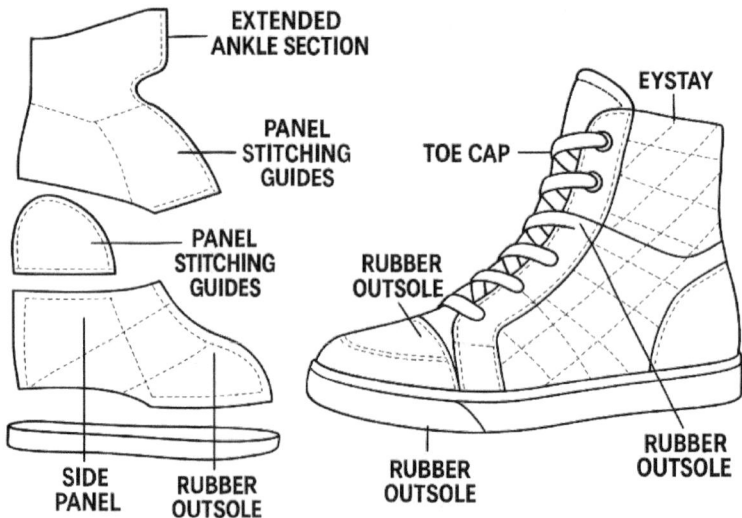

EXTENDED ANKLE SECTION

EYSTAY

PANEL STITCHING GUIDES

TOE CAP

PANEL STITCHING GUIDES

RUBBER OUTSOLE

RUBBER OUTSOLE

SIDE PANEL

RUBBER OUTSOLE

RUBBER OUTSOLE

RUBBER OUTSOLE

Perfect for bold, high-top designs—this template supports extra height and layered quilting with style and structure.

3. Slip-On Sneaker Template

- For those who want to customize a pair of slip-ons, this template takes into account the absence of laces and requires precise fitting for a seamless look.
- **Included:**
  - Simple pattern with fewer parts, ideal for fast projects
  - Suggested quilting patterns for slip-on aesthetics (e.g., minimalist geometric shapes)
  - Special attention to fit around the heel and arch
- **Use for:** Quick customization and testing new fabric types, great for beginner quilters.

Create clean, modern slip-ons fast—this simplified template is ideal for minimalist aesthetics and quick projects.

4. Multi-Panel Quilted Sneaker Template

- This advanced pattern allows you to design quilted sneakers with multiple fabric panels, creating a striking, complex design. This template challenges you to get creative with color blocking, contrasting fabrics, and layered designs.

- o **Included:**
  - Instructions on how to break down a sneaker into several panels
  - Measurement adjustments for creating smooth transitions between fabric pieces
  - Options for detailed embellishments, including embroidery, beadwork, and fabric painting
- o **Use for:** Experienced quilters or those looking to create statement sneakers with intricate patterns.

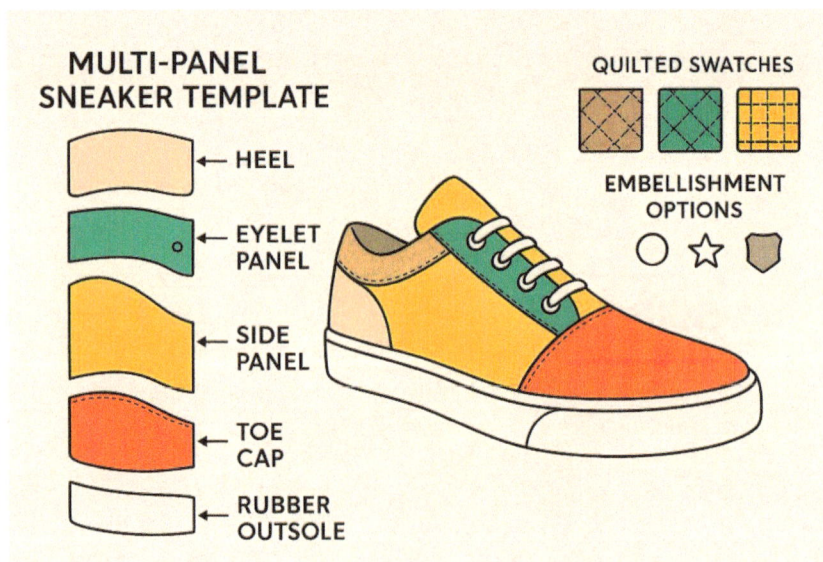

MULTI-PANEL SNEAKER TEMPLATE

← HEEL

← EYELET PANEL

← SIDE PANEL

← TOE CAP

← RUBBER OUTSOLE

QUILTED SWATCHES

EMBELLISHMENT OPTIONS

Get creative with color and texture—this advanced template lets you design standout sneakers with layered panels and artistic detail.

5. **Classic Sneaker Template with Embellishment Zones**

- This pattern is designed for users who wish to add embroidery, patches, or other embellishments to their sneakers. It includes specific zones where these accents will have the most impact.

- **Included:**

  - Templates with pre-marked areas for embroidery or decorative stitching

  - Recommended fabric types for embellishment (e.g., velvet, satin, or denim)

  - Tips for balancing embellishments with the overall design

- **Use for:** Sneakers that need a personal, artistic touch or for quilters looking to showcase their embroidery skills.

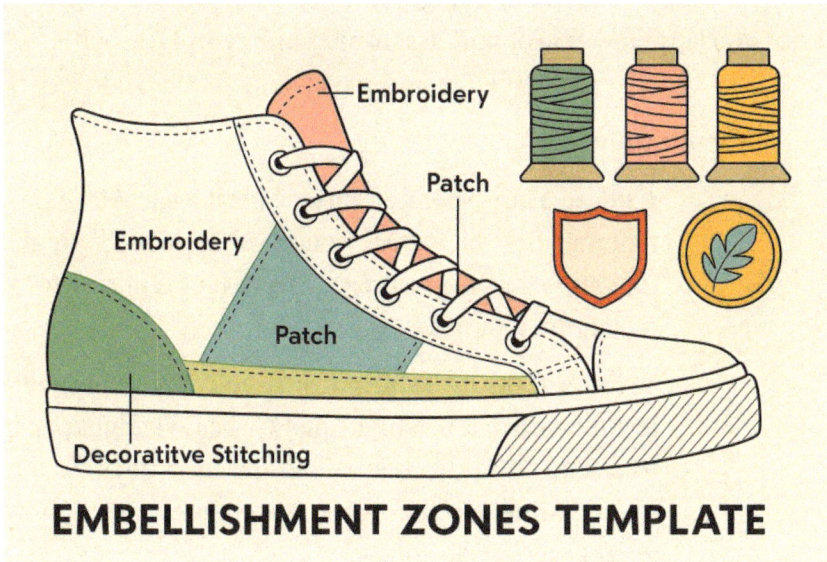

EMBELLISHMENT ZONES TEMPLATE

Showcase your artistic flair—this template highlights key zones for embroidery, patches, and decorative stitching.

~ ~ ~ ~ ~

B. How to Use the Templates

**Follow four key steps to bring your sneaker quilting to life—
choose, print, trace, and assemble your templates with
confidence and precision.**

1. **Preparation**

   o **Choose Your Sneaker Base:** Select a sneaker type
     that matches the pattern you're using (low-top, high-
     top, slip-on). Make sure you have the right size to
     match the template.

   o **Print & Cut the Templates:** If you're working with a
     printed version, use high-quality, heavyweight paper
     to ensure durability. Cut along the solid lines for the
     main outline and follow the dotted lines for stitch
     guides and fabric zones.

   o **Size Adjustments:** For custom fitting, adjust the
     pattern to fit different shoe sizes. You can enlarge or

shrink the templates using a copier or scanning software to match the shoe's dimensions.

2. Transferring the Pattern

- Lay your fabric on a flat surface and use a fabric marker to trace the template onto the fabric. Be sure to add a seam allowance to all edges (typically 1/4 inch) for the stitching process.

- **Tip:** If working with a patterned fabric, ensure that the design aligns with the template for a uniform look once stitched.

3. Quilting with the Templates

- Use the quilting patterns provided within the templates, such as diamond shapes, grids, or creative free-form designs. Each pattern is mapped out with recommended stitch lines to ensure the fabric holds its structure while adding style.

- **Tip:** Use contrasting thread colors to make your quilting pattern stand out or match your fabric for a seamless, professional finish.

4. Sewing & Assembly

- Once the quilting is complete, assemble your quilted panels onto the sneaker base. Follow the instructions for securing each section, and use appropriate adhesives or stitching techniques to hold the panels in place. For multi-panel templates, make sure to stitch one section at a time for a clean, cohesive look.

~ ~ ~ ~ ~

C. Template Variations & Customization Ideas

Denim and velvet

Appliqué overlays
Printed quilting

Fabric patches
with quilt stitching

Contrasting thread
Layered textures

From bold fabric swaps to layered embellishments, one template can lead to endless custom creations—reuse, remix, and make it yours.

- **Creative Additions:** You can modify these templates to add unique flourishes to your designs, such as extra fabric overlays, printed fabric inserts, or layered appliqué designs.

- **Adjusting for Different Styles:** Swap out fabric types (denim, velvet, suede, etc.) or use multiple patterns together for a truly one-of-a-kind look. Play with color gradients, fabric textures, or use contrasting thread for stitching to further personalize the design.

- **Upcycling and Reusing Templates:** The templates are designed for repeated use. Once you've used one for your first set of sneakers, you can use the pattern again with different fabrics or customize it further.

By using these templates, you're setting yourself up for a successful and enjoyable quilting journey, allowing you to craft a personalized pair of sneakers with each step you take.

Appendix B: Complete Resource & Supplier Guide

This section serves as your go-to resource for finding the best materials, tools, and suppliers to help bring your quilted sneaker vision to life. Whether you're looking for premium fabrics, specialty tools, or embellishments to add that extra touch, we've compiled a comprehensive list of trusted brands, online stores, and local suppliers that offer everything you need to start your quilting journey. Use this guide to find the right products, ensure quality materials, and save time sourcing the items that will make your quilted sneakers truly unique.

~ ~ ~ ~ ~

A. Fabric & Materials Suppliers

1. **Fabric.com**

   o Website: www.fabric.com

   o Description: Fabric.com offers a wide range of high-quality quilting cottons, denim, and other fabrics suitable for quilting projects. Their extensive collection includes solids, prints, and textured fabrics perfect for sneaker customization.

   o Notable Features:

      ▪ Free shipping on orders over a certain amount

- Large variety of materials including denim, cotton, and specialty fabrics
- Frequent sales and discounts

2. Joann Fabrics

o Website: www.joann.com

o Description: Joann is one of the largest fabric retailers, offering a vast selection of quilting fabrics, sewing tools, and notions. It's a great option for beginners and professionals alike, with a wide variety of options for customization and sneaker quilting projects.

o Notable Features:

- Convenient online and in-store shopping
- Customizable fabric printing options
- Excellent selection of quilting accessories

3. Spoonflower

o Website: www.spoonflower.com

o Description: Spoonflower allows you to create custom fabrics that can be printed with your own designs. It's an excellent choice for personalizing the look of your quilted sneakers with unique, one-of-a-kind fabric prints.

o Notable Features:

- Print custom designs on various fabric types
- Eco-friendly options
- Global shipping

4. Mood Fabrics

- o Website: www.moodfabrics.com

- o Description: Mood Fabrics is known for offering high-end fashion and quilting fabrics. If you're looking to elevate your sneaker designs with luxurious materials like velvet, satin, or silk, this is the place to go.

- o Notable Features:

  - ▪ Famous for its selection of designer fabrics

  - ▪ Offers unique materials for custom sneakers

  - ▪ Excellent customer service and fabric expertise

~ ~ ~ ~ ~

B. Tools & Equipment Suppliers

1. Wawak Sewing

- o Website: www.wawak.com

- o Description: Wawak offers a comprehensive range of sewing supplies, including quilting tools, threads, needles, and more. It's a great resource for sourcing professional-grade quilting equipment at competitive prices.

- o Notable Features:

  - ▪ Discounted prices for bulk purchases

  - ▪ Fast and reliable shipping

  - ▪ A wide range of sewing tools and supplies

2. The Sewing Studio Fabric Superstore

- o Website: www.sewingstudio.com

- o Description: This store is known for its variety of quilting notions, sewing machines, and fabric. They have everything from rotary cutters and quilting rulers to premium threads, ideal for making your quilting projects precise and professional.
- o Notable Features:
  - Specialty in quilting tools
  - Free shipping on orders over a certain amount
  - Offers sewing classes and tutorials

3. Amazon

- o Website: www.amazon.com
- o Description: Amazon is a convenient place to buy quilting tools, fabric, and supplies. With a wide selection from various brands, you can often find deals and customer reviews that help you make informed purchasing decisions.
- o Notable Features:
  - Vast selection of products
  - Reviews and ratings for each item
  - Convenient shipping and delivery options

~ ~ ~ ~ ~

C. Embellishment & Customization Suppliers

1. Michaels

- o Website: www.michaels.com
- o Description: Michaels is an arts and crafts store that offers a variety of embellishments such as beads, buttons, sequins, fabric paint, and embroidery threads.

Their craft supplies are perfect for adding the finishing touches to your quilted sneakers.

- o Notable Features:
    - Regular sales and discounts on craft supplies
    - In-store pickup options
    - Extensive selection of craft embellishments

2. Beadaholique

- o Website: www.beadaholique.com
- o Description: Beadaholique specializes in beads, jewelry-making supplies, and embellishments. They offer a wide selection of small decorative elements, perfect for adding sparkle, texture, or personalized accents to your quilted sneakers.
- o Notable Features:
    - Wide variety of beads, rhinestones, and other embellishments
    - Detailed tutorials and project ideas
    - International shipping

3. Tandy Leather

- o Website: www.tandyleather.com
- o Description: Tandy Leather is an excellent source for leather embellishments, trims, and supplies. If you want to add a touch of leather to your quilted sneakers, this is the place to go.
- o Notable Features:
    - Wide selection of leather and leatherworking tools

- Custom stamping and engraving options
- Regular leather crafting tutorials

~ ~ ~ ~ ~

D. General Craft & Quilting Resource Guides

1. Craftsy

- Website: www.craftsy.com
- Description: Craftsy is an online platform offering quilting courses, project ideas, and patterns. It's a great resource for learning advanced quilting techniques and finding new inspiration for your sneaker designs.
- Notable Features:
  - Offers video tutorials and online workshops
  - Wide range of quilting and crafting courses
  - Offers free patterns and downloadable resources

2. Quilt Shop Locator

- Website: www.quiltshops.com
- Description: This directory of quilt shops across the country helps you find local stores where you can source fabrics, notions, and other tools for your quilting projects.
- Notable Features:
  - Searchable database of quilt shops
  - Find locations near you
  - Information on store hours, classes, and events

~ ~ ~ ~ ~

E. Troubleshooting & Helpful Resources

1. Quilting Help Forums

- o Website: www.quiltingboard.com

- o Description: Quilting forums like Quilting Board are excellent places to ask questions, get feedback, and connect with other quilters who can offer advice and insights for your projects.

- o Notable Features:

    - Community-driven support

    - Ask questions and share experiences

    - Helpful tips and techniques for solving quilting problems

2. YouTube Quilting Tutorials

- o Website: www.youtube.com

- o Description: YouTube is filled with quilting tutorials from beginner to advanced techniques. You can find step-by-step videos for almost every stage of your quilted sneaker project.

- o Notable Features:

    - Free access to a wide range of quilting videos

    - Learn at your own pace

    - Follow along with visual instructions

~ ~ ~ ~ ~

By utilizing this Complete Resource & Supplier Guide, you'll have the tools and materials at your disposal to craft stunning quilted sneakers. Whether you are looking for the best fabrics, intricate embellishments, or professional quilting tools, these trusted suppliers will help you create a personalized and standout design.

Appendix C: Troubleshooting & FAQs

In this section, we address common issues and questions you may encounter while working on your quilted sneakers. Whether you're a beginner or an experienced quilter, these helpful troubleshooting tips and frequently asked questions will guide you through any obstacles, ensuring your creative process remains smooth and enjoyable. From fabric challenges to stitch problems, we've got you covered with clear solutions and expert advice to keep your project on track.

~ ~ ~ ~ ~

A. Common Troubleshooting Issues

1. **Uneven Stitching**

   o **Problem:** Your stitches are inconsistent, with some being too tight or too loose.

   o **Solution:** Check your needle size and thread tension. Use a thinner needle for lightweight fabrics and thicker thread for heavier materials. Make sure your sewing machine is properly threaded and clean, or adjust your hand-stitching technique to maintain a consistent stitch length.

2. **Fabric Puckering**

   o **Problem:** The fabric is puckering or bunching up around your stitching.

- o **Solution:** This often happens when the fabric is too tight during stitching. Use a walking foot if using a machine, which helps keep the fabric moving evenly. When hand-stitching, ensure that your fabric is well-secured with pins or fabric clips, and use gentle tension when pulling your thread.

3. **Fabric Shrinkage**

- o **Problem:** Your fabric has shrunk after quilting or washing.

- o **Solution:** Always pre-wash your fabrics before starting your quilted sneaker project. This ensures they're properly pre-shrunk. If shrinkage occurs after quilting, carefully press the fabric with steam to smooth it back into shape, or consider using a fabric stabilizer for future projects.

4. **Misaligned Panels**

- o **Problem:** The quilted panels are not aligning properly when sewing onto the sneaker base.

- o **Solution:** Make sure to measure and mark your fabric before cutting. Use fabric clips to secure your panels and ensure they remain straight during sewing. You can also lightly mark alignment lines on your sneaker base to guide panel placement.

5. **Glue Residue or Stains**

- o **Problem:** You notice glue stains or residue on the fabric after applying adhesive to your quilted panels.

- o **Solution:** Use a damp cloth to gently wipe off any excess glue while it's still wet. If the glue has dried, use rubbing alcohol to remove it. For stubborn stains, try a fabric cleaner specifically designed for delicate materials.

$$\sim \sim \sim \sim \sim$$

B. *Frequently Asked Questions (FAQs)*

1. **How can I make sure my quilted sneakers are durable enough for everyday wear?**

   o **Answer:** To ensure your quilted sneakers hold up, use high-quality fabrics and reinforce your stitching. Apply a fabric sealant to protect your work from moisture and dirt. Additionally, select durable fabric types like denim or canvas for the base material to provide extra sturdiness.

2. **What should I do if my fabric doesn't stay in place while I'm quilting?**

   o **Answer:** If your fabric is shifting or not staying in place, try using a basting spray or fabric adhesive to temporarily hold it while you stitch. For better stability, consider using a stabilizing interfacing, which will keep the fabric in place without adding too much bulk.

3. **Can I quilt on any type of sneaker?**

   o **Answer:** While most canvas and fabric sneakers work well with quilting, other materials like leather or synthetic fabrics may require extra preparation or different techniques. For leather or vinyl sneakers, you may need to pre-punch holes or use a specialized needle and thread designed for heavier materials.

4. **How do I add custom embroidery or embellishments to my quilted sneakers?**

o **Answer:** Once you've quilted your panels and attached them to your sneakers, you can add embroidery, beads, patches, or other embellishments. Use embroidery threads and an embroidery hoop to stitch your designs. For fabric embellishments like patches or beads, sew them on carefully using a hand needle or a specialized sewing machine foot.

5. **What is the best way to store quilted sneakers when not in use?**

o **Answer:** To maintain the shape and integrity of your quilted sneakers, store them in a cool, dry place away from direct sunlight. Use shoe trees to help retain their shape and avoid folding or creasing. If you need to store them for a longer period, wrap them in acid-free tissue paper and place them in a dust bag to protect the fabric.

~ ~ ~ ~ ~

C. Advanced Tips for Problem Solving

1. **Dealing with Fabric Edges**

o **Problem:** Fabric edges are fraying or becoming undone.

o **Solution:** Use a zig-zag stitch or a serger to finish the edges of your fabric before quilting. This will help prevent fraying and keep your panels neat. You can also use a fabric stabilizer along the edges to provide extra protection.

2. **Difficulty Matching Thread to Fabric**

o **Problem:** The thread doesn't blend well with your fabric or stands out too much.

- o **Solution:** If you're using a contrasting thread for visual impact, choose a thread color that complements your fabric pattern. For a more subtle effect, select a thread color that matches your fabric closely. Consider using a neutral tone like beige or gray for a seamless look.

3. **Ensuring Even Quilting Across Multiple Panels**

   - o **Problem:** Your quilting design looks uneven across different panels of the sneaker.

   - o **Solution:** To achieve a consistent look, try quilting all panels in one sitting or at least within the same time frame. This ensures that your stitching pattern remains consistent. If working with multiple panels, make sure to measure and mark all stitching lines for a more accurate design.

~ ~ ~ ~ ~

By following these troubleshooting tips and referring to the FAQs, you can overcome common challenges that arise during the quilted sneaker process. Remember, quilting is a learning journey, and each project will build your skills and confidence. With patience and practice, you'll be able to solve problems creatively and enjoy a smooth crafting experience from start to finish.

Appendix D: Glossary of Sneaker Quilting Terms from A to Z

This glossary serves as a comprehensive reference for all the terms you'll encounter during your quilting journey. Whether you're new to sneaker quilting or a seasoned maker, understanding these terms will help you navigate your projects with ease and confidence. Each definition is tailored to the context of quilted sneakers, ensuring clarity and relevance to your creative process.

~ ~ ~ ~ ~

A

- **Appliqué:** A quilting technique where pieces of fabric are sewn onto a larger piece to create a design, often used for embellishing sneaker panels.
- **Assymmetrical Design:** A design that lacks symmetry, creating an intentional, off-center look for a unique, artistic effect on sneakers.

B

- **Batting:** A layer of padding used between quilt panels to provide structure, warmth, and comfort. Common materials include cotton or polyester.
- **Basting:** A temporary stitching or pinning technique used to hold quilt pieces in place before permanent sewing.

C

- **Canvas:** A durable, woven fabric often used as the base for sneakers, ideal for quilting due to its stiffness and durability.
- **Chain Stitch:** A type of embroidery stitch that forms a series of interconnected loops, used to add decorative elements to your quilted sneakers.

D

- **Die-Cut Templates:** Pre-cut patterns made from rigid material like cardboard or plastic, used for accurately cutting fabric pieces to match a pattern.
- **Dyeing:** The process of coloring fabric with dyes to achieve the desired shade for sneaker panels or embellishments.

E

- **Edge Stitching:** A technique where the stitching is applied close to the fabric's edge, often used to secure quilted panels onto sneakers.

- **Embroidery Thread:** A special type of thread used for decorative stitching, usually thicker than regular sewing thread, and available in various colors.

F

- **Fusible Web:** A type of adhesive fabric used to bond materials together, often employed in quilting to attach pieces without sewing.

- **Free-Motion Quilting:** A technique where you move the fabric freely under the needle of a sewing machine to create intricate quilting patterns.

G

- **Grainline:** The direction in which fabric threads are woven. It is crucial to align quilt panels along the grainline for a proper fit and to avoid distortion.

- **Gridded Quilting:** A quilting technique that involves stitching straight lines at regular intervals to create a grid pattern on your quilted sneakers.

H

- **Hexagon Quilt Block:** A six-sided shape used in quilting that can create a honeycomb effect when arranged in a pattern, often used for creating unique sneaker designs.

- **Hand-Tying:** A method of fastening quilted layers together with knots instead of stitching.

I

- **Interfacing:** A material used to reinforce fabrics, providing added structure and stability to quilted panels, especially for sneaker designs that require more firmness.

- **Iron-On Transfers:** Pre-designed patterns that can be transferred onto fabric using heat, ideal for adding designs to quilted sneaker panels.

J

- **Juki Machine:** A popular brand of sewing machines known for their durability and precision, commonly used for quilting projects.

- **Jelly Roll:** A pre-cut bundle of fabric strips, often used in quilting to create designs quickly and efficiently.

K

- **Knotting:** A technique used to fasten fabric pieces by tying threads together, often seen in decorative quilting patterns.

- **Keyhole Stitch:** A decorative stitch that creates a looped effect, typically used for adding intricate details to quilted sneakers.

L

- **Layered Quilting:** A quilting technique where multiple layers of fabric and batting are sewn together, providing depth and texture to your design.

- **Linen Fabric:** A natural fabric made from flax, often used in quilted sneaker designs due to its smooth texture and durability.

M

- **Machine Quilting:** The process of using a sewing machine to stitch quilt layers together, typically faster than hand quilting.

- **Marking Tools:** Tools such as fabric markers, chalk pencils, or water-soluble pens used to trace patterns onto fabric.

N

- **Needle Threading:** The process of preparing a needle with the appropriate thread, a critical step in both hand and machine quilting.
- **Narrow Binding:** The technique of finishing the edges of quilted panels by folding over a strip of fabric, used for a clean, polished look on sneaker edges.

O

- **Overlock Stitch:** A machine stitch used to finish raw fabric edges, preventing fraying and ensuring durability.
- **Ornaments:** Decorative elements like buttons, beads, or sequins that can be added to quilted sneakers for a personalized touch.

P

- **Patchwork:** A quilting technique that involves sewing together small pieces of fabric to create a larger design, often used for colorful sneaker panels.
- **Pinking Shears:** Special scissors with a zig-zag blade, used to cut fabric edges and prevent fraying.

Q

- **Quilt Sandwich:** The combination of the top quilted fabric, batting, and backing fabric, assembled before quilting begins.
- **Quilting Frame:** A structure used to hold quilt layers taut while they are being stitched, often used for hand quilting.

R

- **Running Stitch:** A simple, straight stitch that is widely used for basic quilting designs, ideal for beginner quilters.
- **Reverse Stitching:** A sewing technique used to secure thread at the beginning or end of a seam, ensuring durability.

S

- **Seam Allowance:** The extra fabric on the edge of a quilted panel that ensures seams are securely stitched and allows for adjustments.
- **Selvage:** The finished edge of a fabric that prevents fraying, often trimmed off when cutting quilt panels.

T

- **Thimble:** A small protective device worn on the finger to prevent injuries while hand stitching.
- **Tension Settings:** The adjustments made on a sewing machine to control how tightly or loosely the thread is sewn.

U

- **Underlay:** A piece of fabric or material placed under quilted panels to provide additional support and structure.
- **Upholstery Fabric:** Heavy-duty fabric often used in quilting for sneaker designs that require extra strength.

V

- **Variegated Thread:** Thread that has a color gradient, commonly used in quilting to add visual interest and texture to your projects.
- **Vinyl Fabric:** A synthetic material used in quilting to add a sleek, shiny finish to quilted sneakers.

W

- **Wadding:** Another term for batting, used to add volume and softness to quilted panels.
- **Whipstitch:** A type of stitch that is used for hand-finishing seams or securing edges, typically used for attaching quilted pieces to the sneaker base.

X

- **X-Pattern Quilting:** A quilting design that uses diagonal lines crossing at the center, forming an "X" shape. This can add visual interest to sneaker designs.
- **Xylography:** A form of woodblock printing that can be used for custom sneaker designs, particularly in collaboration with quilting techniques.

Y

- **Yarn Stitching:** A thick, textured stitch used to add depth and dimension to quilted sneakers, particularly for a handmade or rustic feel.
- **Yellowing:** The process of fabric discoloration over time, often caused by improper storage or exposure to sunlight. Prevent this by using appropriate fabrics and care techniques.

Z

- **Zigzag Stitch:** A versatile stitch that can be used for both decorative and functional purposes, such as finishing raw fabric edges or creating textured patterns on quilted sneakers.
- **Zippers:** A closure mechanism that can be added to quilted sneakers for both functional and decorative purposes, often incorporated into high-top sneaker designs.

~ ~ ~ ~ ~

This glossary is a valuable reference tool to ensure that you're familiar with all the terms and techniques you'll encounter throughout your quilted sneaker journey. As you progress, you'll develop a deeper understanding of these terms, allowing you to enhance your designs and expand your creativity.

Appendix E: Quilted Sneaker Inspiration Gallery

In this section, you'll find an exclusive collection of quilted sneaker designs to spark your creativity. These designs showcase a variety of styles, patterns, and embellishments that you can incorporate into your own projects. Whether you're looking for bold geometric patterns, intricate floral designs, or futuristic textures, this gallery will help you visualize the endless possibilities for customizing your quilted sneakers.

Let these quilted sneaker designs spark your creativity—mix, match, and reimagine quilted sneakers that reflect your boldest ideas and personal style.

~ ~ ~ ~ ~

A. How to Use This Gallery:

Use the gallery as your springboard—explore, adapt, and remix designs to create sneakers that are truly your own.

1. **Explore the Designs:**
   Browse through the images in the gallery to see different styles and approaches to quilting sneakers. Each design represents a unique combination of fabric choices, patterns, and embellishments, giving you a broad spectrum of inspiration.

2. **Select a Design to Adapt:**
   Find a design that resonates with you, whether it's the overall look, the quilting technique, or the way specific elements are combined. You can adapt the pattern to suit your own sneaker base and customize it with your preferred fabrics, colors, and embellishments.

3. **Use as a Starting Point:**
   Use the gallery designs as starting points to develop your own ideas. You might decide to reinterpret a design with your

fabric choices or create a completely new pattern by mixing and matching elements from different designs.

4. **Incorporate Innovative Visual Elements:**
   The gallery features bold color gradients, striking geometric patterns, and creative fabric combinations that reflect modern design trends. Draw from these visual ideas to give your quilted sneakers a fresh and contemporary twist.

~ ~ ~ ~ ~

B. Featured Sneaker Designs:

1. **Modern Geometric Pattern**

   o A contemporary look that combines bold lines, angles, and abstract shapes for a striking effect. The design uses contrasting colors to create depth and visual interest.

Sharp lines and bold contrast make geometric quilting a powerful design—balance symmetry with color to command attention.

2. Floral Embellishments

- A soft, feminine design featuring floral patterns with delicate stitching. This sneaker showcases intricate embroidery work and a mix of pastel colors for a charming, artistic look.

Add romance to your sneakers with floral quilting—delicate embroidery and soft colors create an artistic, feminine feel.

3. Denim & Leather Hybrid

- A fusion of casual denim with sophisticated leather accents. This design uses a multi-panel approach, with different textures on the toe box, heel, and side panels for added dimension.

Blend texture and tone—combine denim and leather with quilted panels for a cool, tactile design that bridges casual and classy.

4. **Futuristic Metallics**

   o A bold, futuristic design that uses metallic fabrics and reflective materials. This sneaker incorporates geometric shapes to create a high-tech, modern look.

Step into the future with metallic quilting—shiny fabrics and digital-inspired patterns bring a bold, tech-forward twist.

5. Vintage Patchwork

- o A throwback style featuring patchwork designs with various fabrics such as plaid, denim, and suede. This design embraces a nostalgic aesthetic, combining textures and patterns that evoke a sense of handcrafted authenticity.

Channel vintage charm—combine textured fabrics and patchwork quilting for a handcrafted, throwback vibe.

6. Abstract Art Sneakers

- o An avant-garde design with splashes of color, asymmetrical stitching, and unexpected fabric combinations. This design leans into the artistic freedom that quilting allows, creating a one-of-a-kind sneaker.

Turn your sneakers into a canvas—abstract quilting celebrates color, contrast, and creative freedom with every stitch.

~ ~ ~ ~ ~

C. Tips for Using the Gallery Effectively:

Turn inspiration into innovation—combine styles, personalize with bold fabric choices, and elevate your sneakers with one-of-a-kind embellishments.

- **Mix & Match:** Feel free to combine elements from multiple designs to create a sneaker that is entirely your own. For example, you can take the quilting style from one design and pair it with the fabric choices from another.

- **Personalize Your Designs:** Use the quilted sneaker gallery to help you decide on the best fabric combinations, colors, and quilting techniques for your own sneakers. Let these designs inspire new ideas and approaches that reflect your unique style.

- **Experiment with Embellishments:** Many of the quilted sneaker designs include unique embellishments, like embroidery, beadwork, or appliqué. Consider adding similar details to your own sneakers to make them stand out.

~ ~ ~ ~ ~

This Quilted Sneaker Inspiration Gallery is a creative tool to help you visualize the wide range of possibilities for your own designs. Let it be the spark that ignites your next project, whether you're following a specific design or using it as a springboard for new ideas. Remember, the ultimate goal is to create something uniquely yours, combining techniques and materials to tell your personal sneaker story.

About HowExpert

HowExpert publishes quick 'how to' guides on all topics from A to Z. Visit HowExpert.com to learn more.

About the Publisher

Byungjoon "BJ" Min (민병준) is an author, publisher, entrepreneur, and the founder of HowExpert. He started off as a once broke convenience store clerk to eventually becoming a fulltime internet marketer and finding his niche in publishing. He is the founder and publisher of HowExpert where the mission is to make a positive impact in the world for all topics from A to Z. Visit BJMin.com and HowExpert.com to learn more. John 14:6

Recommended Resources

- HowExpert.com – How To Guides on All Topics from A to Z.
- HowExpert.com/free – Free HowExpert Email Newsletter.
- HowExpert.com/books – HowExpert Books
- HowExpert.com/courses – HowExpert Courses
- HowExpert.com/clothing – HowExpert Clothing
- HowExpert.com/membership – HowExpert Membership Site
- HowExpert.com/affiliates – HowExpert Affiliate Program
- HowExpert.com/jobs – HowExpert Jobs
- HowExpert.com/writers – Write About Your #1 Passion/Knowledge/Expertise & Become a HowExpert Author.
- HowExpert.com/resources – Additional HowExpert Recommended Resources
- YouTube.com/HowExpert – Subscribe to HowExpert YouTube.
- Instagram.com/HowExpert – Follow HowExpert on Instagram.
- Facebook.com/HowExpert – Follow HowExpert on Facebook.
- TikTok.com/@HowExpert – Follow HowExpert on TikTok.

Printed in Great Britain
by Amazon

61771356R00141